Advance Praise

""As women entrepreneurs, it is time to use a brand-new value system that better represents what 'success' truly means for us. Leslie's book, 7 Keys to 7 Figures, gives women the tools to see their core values so that they can create an extraordinary business that serves their life."
—ALI BROWN, FOUNDER OF THE TRUST PRIVATE NETWORK FOR $1M+ WOMEN ENTREPRENEURS, COACH, MENTOR, AND HOST OF TOP PODCAST *GLAMBITION*® *RADIO*

"What is most important as a woman in business is to let your light shine! Discover the innate gifts of your strengths and be comfortable in who you are. You will be the most successful when you create a life and business that fit you, not a life to fit in. In 7 Keys to 7 Figures, Leslie shows you how to create a profitable business as well as a business that serves the life you truly desire."
—HOLLY DOWLING, AWARD-WINNING GLOBAL SPEAKER AND TOP TEN INSPIRATIONAL THOUGHT LEADER

"Leslie Kuster's enthusiasm for teaching business strategies and living the life you deserve is infectious. If you want to learn how to run a successful seven-figure business, stick with Leslie. She's done it and can show you how. She talks the talk and walks the walk."
—PAULA RIZZO, EMMY AWARD-WINNING TELEVISION PRODUCER, BESTSELLING AUTHOR, AND MEDIA TRAINER AND STRATEGIST

"Leslie is the real thing! She brought her business from five figures to multiple seven figures, and in her book, she gives women entrepreneurs of all ages the keys to do it."
—KAREN SALMANSOHN, BESTSELLING AUTHOR AND ENTREPRENEUR

"Part business strategy, part life strategy, 7 Keys to 7 Figures not only gives powerful practical expertise on exactly how to build a successful money-making business, but Leslie balances this with her own personal stories, making this book very human and relatable."
—ALISON LUMBATIS, SEVEN-FIGURE FEMALE ENTREPRENEUR, FOUNDER OF OUTFIT FORMULAS, AND BESTSELLING AUTHOR

"The world needs more women to access their prosperity so they and their families can have the life they truly want. In 7 Keys to 7 Figures, women entrepreneurs of all ages who dream of a million-dollar business will have tools for building a business that gives them independence, empowerment, wealth, and the freedom they dream of."
—MICHELLE BOSCH, CO-CREATOR OF THE LAND PROFIT GENERATOR PROGRAM AT ORBIT INVESTMENTS, LLC

"*Life can feel overwhelming when we're building a business while also juggling family, friendships, and our own health. It takes processes, systems, and, more than anything, mindset. This book will help you step up into powerful leadership of yourself and others so that you can enjoy real wealth.*"
—KATHY FETTKE, CO-CEO OF REAL WEALTH NETWORK

"*It is our vision to help women entrepreneurs by transforming their businesses with visibility and strategy. 7 Keys to 7 Figures gives female entrepreneurs the expertise, guidance, and practical tools women need to do this so they can make more money and have more freedom.*"
—JESSICA RHODES, FOUNDER OF INTERVIEW CONNECTIONS AND MENTOR

"*Real transformation, whether in life or in business, needs to start at the roots. Leslie's book not only offers women entrepreneurs savvy business expertise, but directs women entrepreneurs to look inside themselves to understand the root of what could be holding them back, making this book very human and relatable.*"
—AMY ELIZA WONG, FOUNDER OF ALWAYS ON PURPOSE, AUTHOR, AND EXECUTIVE LEADERSHIP COACH

7 Keys to 7 Figures

7 KEYS TO 7 FIGURES

The Women Entrepreneurs'
Guide to Money & Freedom

LESLIE KUSTER

HOUNDSTOOTH
PRESS

7 KEYS TO 7 FIGURES

The Women Entrepreneurs' Guide to Money and Freedom

FIRST EDITION

ISBN   978-1-5445-3840-2 *Hardcover*

978-1-5445-3838-9 *Paperback*

978-1-5445-3839-6 *Ebook*

To my dad, who taught me to just do it.

To my mom, who gave me the courage.

And to my husband, Heinz, who always knew I could.

CONTENTS

FOREWORD

— KRISTINE CARLSON, CO-AUTHOR
OF THE *DON'T SWEAT THE
SMALL STUFF* BOOKS

First, it is an honor to write this foreword for Leslie Kuster and this wonderful book, which is more than your typical business book. Here's a little background on me and my business journey. I have been an entrepreneur my whole life. I started my career out of college as a graphic designer and grew my business into a team of designers under the company name Kristine Carlson: A Marketing Design Group. Then came marriage, motherhood, and a handful of network marketing companies and direct selling. As my husband, Dr. Richard Carlson, pursued his career as an author and entrepreneur simultaneously, he invited me to write with him after his book *Don't Sweat the Small Stuff* became a massive hit around the globe. We wrote *Don't Sweat the Small Stuff in Love* together, and then I wrote my first solo book, *Don't Sweat the Small Stuff for Women*. Later, I wrote *Don't Sweat the Small Stuff for Moms* and several other bestselling books.

Having sold over 30 million copies from the *Don't Sweat* series and built a brand that became a household name, we entered into the growing digital marketing space, where it's truly an entrepreneur's playground of opportunities for reaching and building relationships with our global community.

When Richard tragically died at forty-five years old, I found myself in a position I had never imagined—without my beloved of twenty-five years and with a shattered heart. The healing of my heart and soul would take time, but managing a high-profile brand couldn't be put off for long. In one life-changing instant, I became a single mother and a widow and inherited our Don't Sweat brand and all the responsibility that came with it.

When I felt ready, I dived into all aspects of the business, drawing on my own entrepreneurial know-how and also implementing the graceful ways of doing business I had learned with Richard. Although I had navigated some of our business with experience, I hired a life and business coach to help give me confidence. He was the first of many to take advantage of me financially at a vulnerable time. Unfortunately, I've had a long and expensive education in hiring the wrong people at a time when I hadn't fully embraced my own capabilities as a businesswoman and brand leader. I discovered haphazardly, through trial and error, who I could be as an entrepreneur. Reading this book would have helped give me the confidence I was searching for in another person.

My friend, it is this certainty that has me so excited that you've chosen this book for yourself. If you allow her to, Leslie will help you save a lot of time, money, and precious energy as you discover your full potential as an entrepreneur. Hindsight had shown me that having the *right* business mentor would have saved me a great deal of time and money and would have resulted in more growth faster. I have come to greatly value the clarity and confidence that working with a knowledgeable and trustworthy guide can provide, whether in the short term or over a longer period of time.

That said, as in many things in life, I would not wish to take advice from anyone who hasn't achieved the kind of success I am looking for. I want to receive guidance from a power-house like Leslie Kuster. I want to know that this same person understands how to overcome the obstacles we face day to day as entrepreneurs. Being your own boss is an amazing freedom, but creating the kind of income to support a family and live the entrepreneur's dream is a huge challenge that comes with ups and downs.

Leslie has lived both lives, understanding the grind of corporate life and longing for the freedom that comes with owning her own business. Leslie can be trusted. Her story of how she left the corporate world and followed the breadcrumbs of inspiration to create her wildly successful Back from Bali business will both warm your heart and fire you up. She'll remind you that you're bigger than any obstacles you may encounter and show you how to achieve the success you know deep down you are capable of.

In this book, Leslie has done a masterful job weaving practical, solid business advice with the inspiration that comes from sharing her own journey—including her own personal struggles along the way to earning multiple seven figures. As with most of us who've achieved financial and business success, Leslie's wasn't an overnight success story. It took true grit, heart, and work to achieve the results she wanted.

Leslie shows us in the coming pages that there are choices and priorities on our time that we must make. Many of our choices will serve us, but not having our priorities in alignment with what we value will come at a cost and could take away from the success that's just around the corner once we get that alignment right.

In *7 Keys to 7 Figures: The Women Entrepreneurs' Guide to Money and Freedom*, Leslie offers tools for success and meaningful how-to business advice that rest on a deep understanding of the psychological components that can keep us stuck and stagnant. In short, she shows us and guides us in how to get out of our own way.

For a long time after Richard died, I operated with the deep belief that I had all the money I needed and my finances were secure. Well, guess what? For many years, I didn't make as much as I could have, and as I said earlier, I used my resources and hired the wrong people. If Leslie's grounded wisdom had been available to me back then, I would have understood how that belief about money stifled me. I would have been much more equipped to reach the next level of success sooner than I did.

I love this book for so many of the wise morsels of insight and true advice that come from experience, but the one chapter that *really* hit me was Chapter 3: The Money Business. As entrepreneurs, we must all overcome our personal obstacles related to money—those internal fears and doubts—in order to achieve the kind of success that gives us the authentic freedom we desire. Leslie's voice in this matter is friendly yet assertive as she coaches us in how to gain what we most want by shedding fear and self-doubt. She shows us how important it is to take a magnifying glass to our deepest beliefs around money. She shouts from the mountaintop, "*I love money!*" Why? Because money is far more than an accumulation of numbers. Money is a conduit of energy that gives us the freedom to live the life we deserve. A life that allows us to be our fully feminine selves as wives, mothers, and business owners—gorgeously complex in our needs, wants, desires, and longings.

As women, we don't wish to live as men in the world of business. We want our feminine selves to thrive as we grow our businesses using our feminine strengths. Leslie Kuster is a fully thriving woman who helps other women entrepreneurs to rise—to unhook from our limiting beliefs, thoughts, and habits that lock the door to the success we yearn to find.

With this much-needed book, Leslie has now paved the way for you to break any imaginary glass ceiling and at any age. Whether you are thirty-five or sixty-five, if you have a strong desire to pursue your dreams, this book will give you a map and all the inspiration you need to turn that vision into reality.

I've learned so much from Leslie in *7 Keys to 7 Figures*, and I know you will too! She is the kind of woman who knows what she most desires and how to get it. She's done the work, and she is sharing all that she has gathered from her experience here in these pages.

I have no doubt Leslie is the woman who will elevate you, change your expectations, and help you grow your business and expand your financial wealth.

Read on and allow this beautiful book to give you wings to soar higher.

Treasure the gifts of life and love.

⁀ Introduction ⁀

WOMEN ENTREPRENEURS ARE THE FUTURE

LESLIE KUSTER
SPRING 2022

Women need freedom. And I mean *lots of it!*

We need freedom to pick up our kids when we want to, earn the money we desire, and take a nap when we feel like it. We need to be able to claim our time, live our lives, and not have a boss or anyone else dictate how we choose to live each day. Every one of us has our own physical and energetic rhythms, and sometimes we just need to rest! (I see you over there on the other side of the page nodding your head in agreement.) We need the freedom to take good care of ourselves and our children and to have the ability to take a deep breath every day, finding moments to enjoy the present. This freedom is the reason why entrepreneurship and being one's own boss is attractive to many women.

And yet, one of the things I've seen in my work with women entrepreneurs is that too many are struggling over their financial situations, even those who have already launched their businesses. Many find the business they've put their heart and soul into is still not giving them the money and freedom they hoped for when they started out.

It is time for the struggle to end.

More than ever before, now is the time for women to rise and fully take the reins when it comes to their money, their work, their happiness, and the freedom to live life on their own terms. Truly, there has never been a more critical time in history for women to be financially empowered and free to live their dreams. In every sector of society, old structures are crumbling before our eyes, which is unnerving, for sure. But now we're getting crystal clear about what no longer works so that we can change what needs to be changed.

- We used to think having a job would give us security. Now we know it doesn't.
- Some of us were raised to depend on a man—father, partner, or spouse—to provide for us. Now we know depending on others is a huge risk.
- We have accepted exhaustion and burnout when working for corporations or other businesses. Now we know that's unacceptable.
- We used to believe self-care and taking downtime were selfish. Now we know they're essential.

THE FEMININE APPROACH TO SUCCESS

The good news is, there is so much opportunity out there for women to create their own businesses. Women entrepreneurs are the future. It's the Wild West, except now we cowgirls are coming into our power! The book you hold in your hands is, in effect, a manual for claiming this power and running with it, all while having the time of your life along the way.

It's simply the way it needs to be because *your happiness matters*.

It's time to take control of your life, your time, and your money. It's time to take 100 percent responsibility for *your* dreams and stop working for someone else's dream.

It's time for your freedom.

Dictating your own hours, working from home, having more time with your kids (if you have any), and having the ability to make a seven-figure income and beyond—each of these can absolutely contribute to a life of freedom. But there are obstacles and pitfalls to be aware of as you proceed.

The sobering fact is that 90 percent of women who own and operate a business generate less than $100,000 per year. And 78.5 percent of women-owned businesses do not survive the first year. The path to succeeding as an entrepreneur is often quite different than we think it will be. There are important principles, perspectives, tools, and insights that aren't traditionally taught, especially those specifically geared toward women. Although there is no shortage of books that teach the fundamentals of business building—such as how to write a business plan, research the market, get funding, leverage your network, and so forth—this book takes a different, more feminine approach. In the chapters to come, I will guide you to define your true yearnings, direct your focus, become an unquenchable learner, master your mindset, and take powerful action that is in alignment with your deepest values. I'll also show you how to slow down and listen to your inner guidance, become resilient in the face of adversity, and be unstoppable in your rise to your fullest potential.

As you move from one chapter to the next, you'll find yourself moving past old doubts and fears and becoming excited to get down to business, more at ease about how to handle challenging times, and deeply optimistic about your future.

IT IS NEVER TOO LATE. REALLY!

If you are concerned your time has passed, that you are too old, or too *anything*—too young, too timid, too technologically inept, too scared, too insecure, too uneducated, too overeducated—I'm here to tell you that you aren't. You can do this—if you want to—by following the keys you are about to learn here.

Although this book is for women of every age, including the twenty-something woman who wants to go straight for entrepreneurial gold, I also speak directly to women in their fifties, sixties, seventies, and beyond because it's never too late to reinvent our lives and actualize long-held dreams.

I know firsthand that building a successful business through entrepreneurship can be the ticket for us to achieve this kind of autonomy and agency over our lives. My story, which I share with you here, is evidence that women truly come into their power after fifty. At the age of fifty-five, I took my clothing brand, Back from Bali, from $50,000 a year in annual revenue to multiple seven figures in annual revenue. Today, I'm parlaying the success of the e-commerce platform I built from the ground up into my work as a mentor to women entrepreneurs worldwide.

Wherever you are in your working journey, if you already have a business and want to up-level it (that was me) and want to make more money (that was definitely me), or whether you have left a job or are considering doing so to start a business, this book will help and guide you. If you want to be an entrepreneur and don't yet have a clear business idea, not to worry. As you read this book, you will get ideas.

Last, if you are feeling frustrated or disappointed in where your business or work life is, please know I really get it. I was exactly where you are now. Now I am thriving in every way. And you will be thriving too!

It's all truly possible. I can't wait to show you how.

I have created several free resources to help you implement the strategies in this book. To access them, please visit https://7keysto7figuresbook.com/reader-extras.

Chapter 1

IT'S NEVER TOO LATE—FROM FAILURE TO SUCCESS

"As long as you're breathing, it's never too late to do some good."
—Maya Angelou

I didn't always have the multiple seven-figure e-commerce business that has given me the money, lifestyle, and freedom I now have. In fact, it was only at the age of fifty-five that things changed for me. While sitting in my tiny office back then, in our modest apartment, I was overcome with a deep disappointment in myself that could no longer be ignored. I could no longer silence the voice that kept insisting on my attention.

Leslie, you could be doing so much better.

You are not living up to your potential.

You are a financial loser.

I felt like a failure and not just any failure: an *old* failure. Yikes! There I was, sitting at my office desk on a cheap IKEA chair, feeling pretty miserable. I could hear the Brazilians on the first floor because they really liked to party (a little too often) with loud music. I could hear the guy across the street who was in a never-ending process of renovation with his loud electric saws—*rrrrrrrrrrrr*. We were living in a little provincial village in Switzerland nobody ever heard of, and I really wanted something to change.

I was in midlife, or rather the later side of midlife, and I felt bad about myself professionally and financially. The money I earned helped pay for some great vacations and a few living expenses, but it did not give me what I was craving. I wanted to make more money. I wanted my husband and I to be able to buy our dream apartment. I wanted to have more financial freedom. I wanted to feel independent, where I could afford to take care of myself and live how I wanted. I really wanted all of this, but I didn't have it. I felt stuck and didn't know how to get unstuck.

All I did know was that I didn't want this feeling anymore. I didn't want to feel like a loser. I didn't want to feel like life was passing me by. I didn't want to feel I wasn't living up to what I knew I was capable of. And yet I wondered, *How can I change this? What do I do? Can I change at my age? Isn't it too late?*

It was an ugly moment, one of those "dark nights of the soul" afternoons. I could have temporarily covered it up with chocolate, or shopping, or watching a show, or even with trying to convince myself that success and money were not that important. But unfortunately (or fortunately, depending on how you want to look at it), I had a roaring lion inside of me screaming so loudly that I couldn't help but hear it.

Angry lion seethed at me, insisting I answer its call. "What are you doing with your life? It's time to wake up and change if you want something to change."

Worst of all, it said, "You know you are going to die one day."

That one really got me. In a flash, I saw myself at every age, reaching all the way back to the beginning. Esy Duny (pronounced *Eh-see Doony)* was my baby name. Apparently, when I was three years old, I could not pronounce Leslie June and it came out sounding like Esy Duny. My husband, Heinz, knew how much I wanted a beautiful new apartment, and he would often say to me, "One day, I'm going to build you the Esy Duny tower." That was code for "One day, I will buy you your dream home."

As I sat there in my misery, I realized I needed to build my own Esy Duny tower! Like the princess in the tower waiting for Prince Charming to rescue her, I realized I too had been waiting to be saved. I was waiting, just like many of us women do, for a man to save me from every danger and buy me exactly what I wanted. Waiting for myself to change was no longer an option. I knew unless I changed something myself, nothing else was going to change, at least not in a positive way. I realized it was all up to me, and it was time to stop waiting. It was a sobering moment.

Yet in my moment of despair, I heard my own voice yell out, strong and clear.

"There is no way I am waking up on my next birthday making the same amount of money. There is no way I am not going to live up to my potential. No way!" I roared.

Change often starts this way. We need to get uncomfortable in order to make any big changes in our lives. Each of us humans is similar: we complain and complain about how much we want things to change, and yet we do our best to make sure nothing ever changes through our lack of action and negative thinking. It is only when we are in a corner, emotionally speaking—when we lose a job, get sick, get divorced, or experience some other kind of loss—that we change. In my case, the urgent call to change was coming from inside of me. I could no longer ignore the pain this pattern of waiting and wishing was causing me.

It reminded me of another time in my life, when I was thirty-seven years old, separated with no children, and wanting my personal life to change. I wanted to find my real soul mate. I was feeling lonely and sad living in New York City without a partner when I heard about a weeklong retreat all about "finding your bliss again." I decided to do it. As I walked down the stairs in my apartment building on my way to the workshop, I remember thinking, *There is no damn way I am walking back up these stairs feeling the same way I feel now with all this sadness and loneliness. There is NO WAY I am NOT going to change.*

That is exactly how I felt sixteen years later sitting in my little office listening to the Brazilians partying. I now was in a beautiful, happy marriage with my Swiss man, Heinz, but it was my career and financial life that needed changing. There was no way I was going to continue to feel this pain of not making it, of not earning what I knew I could earn, of playing small, of pretending I didn't really want more. For me, *more* meant fully stepping into my power and independence. More meant pushing myself, learning, and implementing what I had learned so I could build a successful business I didn't only love but that was also a mirror reflecting who I knew I really was.

I had to get honest with myself—really honest.

What rose within me was this: I WANT MONEY! Listen, I know that doesn't sound so politically correct. It's not something you are supposed to say out loud, and it's certainly not ladylike. Women are expected to say they want to help, they want to give, they want to support their families, they want to change the world—not that they want money (not publicly, anyway). But damn it, I wanted money!

I already was an entrepreneur. I came from a family of entrepreneurs. My dad had his own stockbroker placement company and was also a humanistic photographer, capturing the nuanced and poignant moments of people's lives. My mom created her own party planning business and then did real estate investing. I grew up being told to always work for myself. Since I was thirty years old, that is what I had done. I was brought up to value being self-employed over working for a corporation. Being an entrepreneur came naturally to me. Being a successful entrepreneur was another thing.

From the outside, I looked pretty successful. I had two businesses, but between both of them, I was earning only around $68,000 a year. I did have freedom, however. I could work from home. I didn't have a boss telling me how long I could take a coffee or lunch break or when I could go on a vacation. I was able to make my own hours and work at 1:00 a.m. if I wanted to (I never did want to, as I'm not a night person, but I could have). I had the freedom to wake up when I wanted, to take a nap when I wanted, and to run my days as I wanted. But these freedoms alone, as much as I valued them, were no longer enough. There was something missing.

There in my humble office, in this moment of reckoning, I understood what was missing: it was having the courage to allow myself to become successful. What was missing was having the guts to say (through my actions and my words), *I am of value, I am powerful, I am smart, I am capable, I am independent, I am strong. I can stand on my own feet. I do not need someone else to make this happen for me—not a partner, not a husband, not a father to make me feel safe. I can do this on my own.*

I noticed that the operative words were "I am" and "I can." These are two of the most empowering phrases I know. Encoded within them is the deep recognition and acknowledgment of this miraculous life I've been given—one to be lived with passion, aliveness, and joy.

Such a realization creates a moment when we truly grow up and take 100 percent responsibility for our money, our relationships, our homes, our jobs, our businesses, and our happiness. We no longer dim our light so we can be safe or comfortable and continue to lie about what we really want. As Ali Brown, one of my most cherished mentors, describes it, "It's time to put on the big-girl panties."

It was clearly time for me to do this.

Right then and there, I decided I was going to put 100 percent of my effort into my business—to grow it, make real money, and be successful in the ways that mattered to me. I decided that by the following year, I was going to be in a different place and committed to making over $100,000. I made the decision that changed everything: I wanted this, I was going to do this, and nothing was going to stop me.

At that time in 2011, my business, Back from Bali, an e-commerce women's bohemian-style clothing brand, was already selling on Amazon and through my website. It had garnered a modest $50,000 in revenue that year. But that was all about to change.

The next year, it doubled to $100,000.

By 2013, my sales revenue hit $235,170.

In 2014, it climbed to $407,630.

In 2015, it rose to $738,939.

In 2016, it jumped to $954,082.

In 2017, it went over the $1 million mark to $1,202,561 (that was thrilling!).

In 2018, it reached $1,626,452.

At the time of this writing, I have surpassed multiple seven figures. It took me five years to get to $1 million and only another two years to surpass $2 million. And I know many women who have accomplished this much faster than I did.

When I decided to write this book, I kept asking myself, how did I do this? In fact, as I sit here day after day writing, I keep asking myself the same question. How the heck did I manage to do this? How in the world did I end up with a multiple seven-figure business, which has given me both freedom and money? I was no techy, no business genius; I mean, I majored in theater at the University of Colorado and have a master's degree in clinical social work. How does all that compute?

Was it timing? Was it Amazon? Was it my business consultant? Was it luck? Perhaps it was a bit of all those things, although Oprah says there is no such thing as luck—that luck is when opportunity and action meet. Upon reflection, I realized the successes I had resulted from certain actions, behaviors, and beliefs that I implemented and lived by. It is those specific actions, behaviors, and beliefs that now make up the seven master keys to success you are about to learn in this book.

But before I hand you the keys, we need to talk about two important things. The first is your definition of success and freedom, and the second is your relationship with money. These are the foundations on which you will build your business, and they are essential to your success. Don't worry, I'll lead you through all of this!

By the way, Heinz and I now live in the Esy Duny tower, our dream home, and so can you! You can have anything you want. I am about to show you exactly how.

THE FREEDOM BUSINESS

"The greatest lesson of life is that you are responsible for your life."
—OPRAH WINFREY

Before I became an entrepreneur, I hated Sunday nights. I would feel this dread come over me with the thought of commuting and working nine to five. I especially hated it in the summer when I had to leave the beach or mountains on a Sunday afternoon to be back in time to go to work on Monday morning. While sitting in the Hamptons jitney bus, mentally preparing to head back to the city from a beach weekend, I'd wish I was going in the other direction. Even back then, I was craving freedom—freedom to set my own hours and freedom to be where I wanted to be. But, at that time, I just didn't know how to create the kind of freedom I was yearning to have.

When I was in my mid-twenties, I was working as a receptionist for an incredibly energetic and self-assured woman who ran a holistic health business. As I sat at my desk in the dark entryway of a New York City office building without windows, answering phone calls and barely able to leave my seat so I didn't miss a call, I watched Anne come and go as she pleased. She would arrive at any time of the day and stay for a few hours or less. Sometimes she would come in at 11:00 a.m. and stay until 4:00 p.m.; sometimes she would arrive at 1:00 p.m. and stay until 3:00 p.m. And then there were times she would just come in for an hour. I was astonished, as I had never witnessed such a thing before. *How does she do this*, I wondered, *and still run a thriving business?* She literally had no set hours. As I sat at my desk from nine to five making $10 an hour at that time, I was fascinated with how she orchestrated her work life. One day, I got up the courage to ask what her secret was.

"Anne, how do you do this? How do you create the freedom to come and go when you want to?"

Without a moment of hesitation, she said, "You just do it."

Just do it!

Her words had a profound effect on me. It was the first time I considered the possibility that I actually had a *choice.*

Women: we want to choose a life where we love Sunday nights *and* Monday mornings—a life in which waking up is the best part of the day! Zig Ziglar, one of the world's most celebrated motivational speakers and author of one of my favorite books, *See You at the Top,* had an exuberant morning ritual. As he jumped out of bed each day, he would say out loud, "Boy, oh boy, what a wonderful day with lots of opportunity." I know this sounds corny, but give it a try. I've been doing it for years, and it makes me giggle almost every time. Starting my day with a genuine smile and positive expectations is a part of my success recipe.

We want a life that makes us feel, more often than not, like jumping out of bed in the morning. It's a sign we're living a life of our choosing. According to *Entrepreneur* magazine, one of the top reasons people become entrepreneurs is to have the freedom to set their own hours. This is not surprising. Humans crave freedom; it is an essential part of who we are. Many of us don't respond well to being controlled, whether it's having to be in the office at a required time, even if working remotely from our home office, or having someone else determine how much money we can earn in a week, a month, or a year. Time freedom is intimately connected to money freedom. We want to have the means to take our family out for dinner when we're sick and tired of cooking day after day, or the ability to take a day to spend with our child if they're not feeling well or simply need some extra attention and care. It is for reasons like these that women decide to become entrepreneurs—so they get to decide, so they have control. If you've ever worked a nine-to-five job (and I bet you have), I'm sure you can relate and agree these are good reasons, indeed.

THE ENTREPRENEUR'S TRAP

Making the transition from employee to entrepreneur can get tricky, however. It is a shift that calls on us to be mindful of how we're proceeding. We don't want to trade in one form of slavery—working for someone else who controls the amount we make and what we do with our time—to become a slave driver to ourselves. We don't want to be the capable and talented entrepreneur who is drowning in stress, exhaustion, and overwhelm. Believe me, I have at times fallen into this myself, and my husband, Heinz, has shaken me out of my slave-driver mentality by telling me to stop being such a "tough boss" to myself.

The old joke that an entrepreneur is someone who works eighty hours a week for themselves so they don't have to work forty hours a week for someone else is unfortunately true. To become successful, you do have to work hard. But—and this is important—*not all the time.* Throughout this book, I will show you how to build a business that serves you, not one that you serve.

Don't you love the way that sounds? How does it make you feel? Your business serves you; you are not an employee of your business. There is no evil boss watching your every move. Instead, you are telling that business what to do and when you want to hear from it. Once you get that idea firmly planted in your head, you will begin to see things differently. You are then on your way to creating a business that gives you freedom.

In fact, however you define freedom for yourself (financial freedom, lifestyle freedom, creative freedom, or otherwise), I encourage you to make freedom your mascot—a powerful symbol reminding you of why you started your business in the first place, or why you're planning to start one soon.

It took a while, but I found out for myself how crucial this declaration of freedom is and continues to be over time.

DROWNING IN MY BUSINESS

Ali Brown, who I mentioned earlier, is one of my mentors, and if you don't yet know who she is, you are in for a treat. Ali is the world's most recognized coach for women entrepreneurs, host of the acclaimed *Glambition® Radio* podcast, and founder of The Trust, the new private network for $1 million-plus women entrepreneurs. A few years ago, I went to one of Ali's workshops in Arizona and was blown away by what I learned. I met several of her students, women who were running multiple seven-figure businesses and working only a few hours a week. Notice I said *a week*, not a day! Just like when I was a receptionist in New York, I was determined to know how they were accomplishing this magical feat.

At the time, I was working far too much and doing many things for my business that I didn't really like and, frankly, was not great at. I finally had to admit to myself that I was starting to dislike my business because I felt burdened. As I sat day after day behind my computer screen—often working until 9:00 p.m. and on weekends—I felt further and further away from the free-spirited woman I knew I was. I felt buried alive under the weight of my to-do list and found myself fantasizing about selling my business and getting out completely. Where was the freedom that I created this business for in the first place? What happened to it? Could I find it again?

Here is an entry from my journal at that time:

I've hit a wall. I feel overwhelmed and miserable in my business; there is just too much to do. I am drowning in this job right now. I feel tired, I feel sad, and I feel that my inspiration has evaporated.

Needless to say, this is not a good place to be as a business owner. It's the kind of misery that leads to giving up.

My business is called Back from Bali. The women's bohemian-style clothing I create is ethically made by women and their family-owned businesses in Bali, Indonesia. Yep, I get to go to Bali for work! That part of my business is incredibly fun. I peruse fabric stories and choose beautiful patterns. I then work with my manufacturers to design colorful, flowing, warm-weather clothing. And I often end my workdays there watching the sunset on the beach while sipping a coconut. Not bad!

But there is another part of the business I run: I am in the e-commerce business. I sell my line of clothing on Amazon and through my own website. In order to have success online, I need to know about keywords and SEO (search engine optimization), digital marketing, and all the myriad details that result in top page ranking. Over time, I have learned a great deal. When you type "sarongs for the beach" into the Amazon search bar, the sarongs I have hand-selected in Bali appear on page one.

I thoroughly enjoy spending time in Bali (my home away from home) and overseeing the many activities around the manufacturing of original clothes for women. But at the time of Ali's workshop, the e-commerce part of the equation was weighing on me. When it came to keyword research, managing pay-per-click ads on Amazon, and reviewing reports on page views and ranking, I was feeling unhappy and frustrated. In part, I felt overwhelmed doing this because the Amazon e-commerce world changes fast, requiring you to be on top of it all the time. I just didn't want to spend all my working time in that world.

Also and more to the point, I really didn't like it. It's a whole world of data analysis that is essential to my business, but I had to get honest with myself—it didn't make me want to jump out of bed in the morning proclaiming, "Boy, oh boy, it's a wonderful day with lots of opportunity, and I can't wait to see my page ranking!" Rather, these kinds of activities made me want to crawl under my covers and hide like a crab under a rock. But being the hardworking entrepreneur I am, I slogged through it. I mean, isn't that a cornerstone of having your own business—doing things you don't like and pushing through? The people who push and push and never quit are the successful ones, I thought. But are they?

After coming back from Ali's workshop, I decided I had to change *something*. If the women I met who run companies earning up to $5 million in annual sales could work far fewer hours than me and work only on what they enjoyed, I could surely do it with my $1 million a year in sales, which was what I was bringing in at that time. I didn't think it was possible before the workshop, but when I returned, I thought, *Hmm, maybe it is possible.* I now had proof!

FROM BREAKDOWN TO FREEDOM

When I returned home, I opened an Excel spreadsheet and made a list of every task needed to operate my business—all 200 of them. Next to each task, I wrote the name of the person who actually did the task. When I looked it over, "Leslie" was the name that appeared most often. In fact, my name dominated the spreadsheet. There it was in black and white—the reason I had been feeling so overwhelmed and unhappy at times with my business. I had become an employee of Back from Bali, and it turned out that my boss (also me) was a demanding tyrant!

This called for further investigation and truth-telling.

Next, I highlighted the tasks for myself that met two important criteria: (1) things that only I could do and (2) things that I like to do. This included the following:

1. Traveling to Bali
2. Sourcing the clothing (including fabrics and patterns)
3. Working with my vendors
4. Overseeing photo and video shoots
5. Managing the money and reviewing the profit and loss statements
6. Managing the overall strategy and direction of my business
7. Continuous learning, especially through podcasts, online courses, and hiring mentors for expert guidance

These are the tasks I love to do. So why was I the person downloading reports, which also required deleting unneeded information from the reports before reviewing them? Why was I the one manually adding the products that shipped from Bali into Amazon's shipment plan? Why was I creating the barcode stickers needed for each of my products and emailing them to my operations manager in Bali?

Truthfully, before this point, I'd simply never asked myself why I would spend my energy this way. It's just what I did based on my work ethic. But during Ali's workshop, a simple yet profound change occurred. Ali made the radical recommendation that we only do what makes us happy in our businesses, rather than what might make us more successful.

Am I really allowed to put happiness over success, my beaten-down employee self wondered?

Over the next year, I hired my business mentor to also handle the e-commerce tasks I don't like and am not really good at—someone who is brilliant at online sales and marketing and, more importantly, who loves it. I also turned over many of the tasks I had been doing to my virtual assistant, giving her a pay increase and bonus in the process.

One year later, I found myself in love with my business again and working only five to twenty hours per week. And get this: The following year was when my business hit *multiple* seven figures.

The year I worked less was the year my business grew even more.

In full disclosure, this happened after being in business for six years and working really hard to build it up. It might not be possible to delegate or outsource in this way at the beginning stages of growing a business. (Although who am I to tell you it isn't? Maybe you'll prove me wrong, and I hope you do.) The point is, what may start out as an asset (like working hard and being responsible for all or most tasks) can become a liability if you aren't prepared to change. I had fallen into the trap of believing I had to do it all, do work I didn't really like, and work long hours week after week. But I'm no longer trapped at all and can now give you the good news: You don't have to fall into the trap—ever! And if you've already fallen in, I'm here to help you out.

There are many entrepreneurs before me who have discovered how working less does not actually mean earning less. Probably the most famous among them is Tim Ferris, author of *The 4-Hour Work Week*. In his bestselling book, Tim teaches you how to escape the nine-to-five grind and outsource much of the work you do. Kate Northrup's book, *Do Less: A Revolutionary Approach to Time and Energy Management for Busy Moms*, speaks directly to women about how doing less doesn't mean creating less or earning less. I love these messages of freedom, empowerment, and being at choice.

WHOSE WORK ETHIC IS IT ANYWAY?

We often forget we even have a choice when it comes to how much we work. One reason we forget is because of our "strong work ethic" culture that praises those who work long hours and undervalues those who work less. Being married to a European man, I've had the opportunity to see another way of working up close and personal. Most people in Europe receive five to six weeks of paid holiday time every year. Somehow, my brilliant husband has managed to get even more paid leave, often taking ten weeks off per year. I've always been impressed with how he has managed to do this, but I must also admit there were times when I bumped up against my American conditioning and needed to check my own judgments at the door.

When I was able to get my multiple seven-figure business to

run on five to twenty hours a week (something I didn't believe was possible until it was), I remember feeling guilty telling my business mentor. There was that trap again! It was clear to me that even though we can say we want more free time and more income (and we do), some of us have to confront our addiction to work, which often includes a lot of complaining about how much we have to work.

Can you relate to this? Do you derive just a bit of masochistic enjoyment from complaining about how much you have to do and how hard you work? If so, you're not alone. Many of us get caught in the habit of thinking that the more we work, the more value we will appear to have. We believe the more we push—the more effort we exert—the more successful we will be.

But our work life can be different. We don't have to remain loyal to these beliefs any longer. We don't have to believe that being a slave to our business is the only way to build a successful one. We don't have to believe that being exhausted is the mark of a real entrepreneur.

The way to leave these beliefs behind is to decide what your endgame is. Decide what freedom means to you. Decide what success—*authentic success*—means to you. Your deepest personal definitions and decisions in these areas will become your guiding principles and will help you live the life you want to live each day. Your greatest freedom will come from the decision and choices you are willing to make.

You can free yourself from the status quo of what a successful entrepreneur is supposed to look like and get into the driver's seat. *You* get to decide what *your* success looks like, and it might look different than what you thought it would or should.

Let's get specific.

YOUR AUTHENTIC SUCCESS

Suppose success looks different than what you have been traditionally taught. In addition to having all the money you want, suppose it also includes more downtime, alone time, self-care time, and family time. Maybe it includes giving financial support to a cause you believe in, moving someplace where you can live a simpler life and grow your own food, or pursuing a creative dream such as painting, singing, or writing.

Suppose *you* decided. And suppose that whatever you decided is the right answer!

The answers you come to naturally and enthusiastically define your *authentic success*, and that is the success I encourage you to follow because it will lead you not only to money and freedom but to happiness. As you inquire into what authentic success means to you, what do you hear or feel from deep within yourself? What does your typical day, week, month, or year look like? Does it mean having a certain amount of income? Is it being able to spend three full days a week with your kids? Does it mean working a certain number of hours per week or per day? Is it creating a large business that provides good jobs for others? What is it that makes success meaningful to you and brings it fully to life, rather than being a word written on a page? Whatever your answers are, you want your business to give rise to your definition of freedom and success, which is why you started your business in the first place!

A reminder: Be as discerning and honest with yourself as you can be when taking inventory this way. It's easy to be seduced into working for the ego's ideas of success, which can have you overfocusing on things like the kind of car you drive, the neighborhood you live in, the school you send your children to, the number of awards or accolades you receive for your work, or your gross salary or gross sales revenue.

I used to get hung up on my gross yearly sales revenue, or the total sales I do before subtracting all the expenses it takes to get those sales. But the truth is, those sales revenues mean nothing, except to the ego. All that really matters is the net—the number *after* subtracting those expenses. It is the net, actually, that gives you the means to your freedom.

Mike Michalowicz, author of *Profit First*, taught me to always pay myself first (thank you, Mike), and by implementing his brilliant system, I always have the money to pay my taxes. What a relief! In his book, Mike tells his own life-changing story. On the outside, he looked like a super successful owner of several businesses, replete with a luxurious house and car. But the truth was, he was in a dire financial situation, close to bankruptcy and unable to pay all of his bills. One evening, Mike confessed all of this to his family at the dinner table. His daughter, who was nine years old, got up and returned with her piggy bank, handing it to her dad. With a palpable vulnerability, he writes, "You know you've hit financial rock bottom when your nine-year-old daughter offers up her piggy bank to bail you out." This was Mike's turning point, where he stopped focusing on his top line sales revenue instead of what he got to keep.

During the COVID-19 pandemic that started in early 2020, my sales revenue dropped in the first three months—or more accurately, it plummeted like a runaway elevator in a movie. It made me seriously question myself. *If I am no longer a multiple seven-figure entrepreneur, who am I?* I wondered. My identity was attached to that label, especially the *multiple seven-figure* part. The experience forced me to acknowledge, once again, that focusing only on sales revenues does not show the true health of a business, nor the true happiness and satisfaction of the owner. I knew that the profit in my pocket, which supports my freedom, was my real goal and that focusing on protecting it instead of the overall sales was of greater importance. Thankfully, my clothing is affordable and comfortable for women to wear at home, which is where almost everyone was confined to at that time. Between that and lowering some expenses, my business recovered.

If I had focused only on getting those sales numbers up so I could brag about them to others (and to myself), I would have fallen into the trap of fake success instead of authentic success. I'm grateful I didn't go down that road. Knowing what freedom and authentic success mean to you will keep you from getting sidetracked as well. Getting clear on why you started your business and how you want that business to serve your life will help you stay on course, as will focusing on your top line happiness and the actual profits in your pocket instead of your top line revenue. These are the things that will give you your freedom.

It's okay if you can't yet see the big picture of what you want your business to do or if some of the details haven't come fully into view. I had no idea years ago that I would have the particular kind of business I now have and the tremendous financial success I enjoy today, but I always knew the lifestyle I wanted to live. I also always knew freedom was important to me. It's the primary reason I now live the life I dearly love, and it will always be the big why that helps me stay on course. Anytime I get off track, as I had before the Ali Brown workshop, I course correct myself back to my commitment to freedom.

Consider once again what authentic success and freedom mean to you—not what they mean to your mom or dad, or your partner, or your best friend, or to those you follow on Facebook and Instagram. What do they truly and honestly mean *to you*? Dig deep down into your heart, into your true self, and ponder these questions for yourself:

What does freedom mean to me?

What is my definition of authentic success?

Why am I an entrepreneur?

I encourage you to make living your freedom and following your authentic success your overriding mantra. If you make them your purpose, your business won't feel like another burden on your shoulders. You'll have it in perspective—seeing your business as a support structure for the life you want to live and the value you want to give to your customers, clients, and the people in your life.

I used to teach a workshop called How to Start an Amazon Business and Make Money Anywhere (which I'll tell you more about later). In this workshop, I would explain how essential it is to have Amazon pick, pack, and ship your products through their Fulfillment by Amazon service so that you don't have to schlep to the post office and mail out your orders. I would tell my workshop attendees, "You don't want to be in the shipping business; you want to be in the freedom business!" And you—you wonderful woman entrepreneur—don't ever forget that is the business you are in too.

But there is one more business you are in as well. Turn the page to find out!

Chapter 3

THE MONEY BUSINESS

"Money…which is hardly spoken of in parlors without an apology, is, in its effects and laws, as beautiful as roses."
—RALPH WALDO EMERSON

Once decided I was committing to my success, I immersed myself in money-making books and audios. I was listening constantly—while driving to Zurich, picking up apples in the grocery store, working out to my Beachbody On Demand videos, and on flights to Bali for my business. Basically, everywhere I went I was listening to the business gurus give their tips for success.

At one point, twelve words stopped me in my tracks. I was walking down the streets of New York City during Thanksgiving week. It was already getting cold, and I buttoned up my coat as I came out of the subway. I took out my phone, put on my headphones, and pushed play. The words of the finance expert came booming through. He said, "If you want to *have* money, you actually need to *want* money."

What he was teaching was so simple and yet so powerful. He was saying you have to consciously want money in order to have money. Those twelve little words woke me up out of my money slumber and began to skyrocket the success of my Back from Bali business. They offered a new way of understanding money that was shimmering with clarity.

What was the new understanding? That we entrepreneurs are in the money-making business!

Having money is what will enable you to have authentic success and freedom. In order to *have* it, you have to *want* it. What a concept!

Just as important, you have to literally be comfortable loving money. Let me say this again: if you want to have money, you have to really WANT and LOVE money. Love, love, love money. I adore the title of Kate Northrup's book on money and women; it's appropriately named, *Money, a Love Story*—because the truth is, you need to have a love affair with your money if you really want to have it. Thank you, Kate!

Know from the beginning that if you want the kind of freedom your business can give you, it IS about making money. You need to say with all honesty that you want money and not only want it but love it. You can kiss that money all over, you love it so much!

By now you're either feeling intrigued, curious, liberated, embarrassed, horrified, or disgusted. You may be lit up with excitement or cringing. Whatever reaction you are having, I am not backing down because this is one truth you need to know right from the start. A real business IS about the money, and if you do want to earn a lot of it, you need to face your own relationship with money.

Oh, damn, you might be saying, *I prefer the part about living my freedom!* I get it. But know this: only when you get totally honest with yourself about the cobwebs of past fears, family beliefs, and societal beliefs about money—and in particular your beliefs about earning money—will you be able to remove those cobwebs and watch the money river flow.

When Desiree Steinmann, who runs a coaching and training business, first decided to open shop, she was a young mother. She knew early on it was important for her to work; however, she and her husband decided he would be the primary bread-winner. Desiree's desire was to be a great mom and at the same time have a business so that when the kids left home, she would already be established in her work.

She said she had never felt drawn to money because it was simply not her focus—until her husband, Peter, lost his job. At first, she was hoping he would get another job soon to replace the lost income. She was operating her small business and taking care of the kids, and she was raised to put the kids first and depend on her husband's income. But then she began to question her beliefs and asked herself, *Why in the world am I putting all the financial pressure on Peter?*

Desiree had a major realization: instead of seeing herself as a mother who had a business, she now saw herself as a businesswoman who had a family. It was a totally new way of looking at her life, her family, and her business. She realized, as a businesswoman, that making money was important so that she could take care of her family. She made a conscious decision to take the sole financial burden off the shoulders of her husband and put it on herself. Then something miraculous happened.

She said, "After making that decision, over the next few months I doubled my income, and this went on for the next few years! The amazing part," she excitedly explained, "was that it was totally effortless. Once I took ownership of making money for our family and decided to become a real businesswoman, everything shifted."

What happened with Desiree is profound. She shifted her attitude and took responsibility for earning money for her family. In response to that decision, she started to earn more—almost like magic. She stepped into her power and realized that earning money was actually a service to her family.

Melinda Gates says, "When money is put into the hands of women, everything changes." Earning more money enables women to take better care of their families and themselves. It allows them to choose to support movements and charities they believe in, and it gives them the fuel to step into the life they want.

Farnoosh Torabi, personal finance expert, writer for *O, The Oprah Magazine*, and podcast host of *So Money* (a fabulous podcast, by the way), says wealthy women can transform the world. She cites research showing that at virtually all income levels, female-headed households (with women who are single, divorced, or widowed) donate more money to charity than male-headed ones. In fact, 64 percent of online donations to charities are made by women because women are givers.

That means earning money is not just good for you; it is good for the world! For many women, to know that earning can help others—either their families or the greater good—makes them feel less guilty about wanting money. But I want you to know, deep down inside your soul, that you are a very good person, a wonderful, kind person, the kind of person you want to be proud of, even when you also allow yourself to say you want money *for you* and you love money *for you*.

STAND UP AND SHOUT

Women, it is time to stand and shout, "I want money!" and not cringe while you say it—not be embarrassed or afraid of appearing greedy. Generating your own money enables you to step into your feminine power, be independent, take care of your family, and enjoy having greater influence on the world around you. Money gives you real wealth—the ability to stand on your own feet and be the director of your life.

Best of all, money gives you the opportunity to have freedom. Notice I said the *opportunity* to have freedom; it doesn't necessarily hand you freedom on a silver platter. But it can create the conditions and circumstances that lead to a life of freedom—and freedom is what it is all about. Remember, you are in the freedom business!

I understand it might feel weird, uncomfortable, and politically incorrect to say you want and love money. Women are generally not taught to go out and make money and be comfortable with making it. We are taught, more often than not, to get a career, work hard, marry or partner well, and secretly hope the money will follow. But it certainly is not something we should publicly or even privately go after and say we want.

I can't tell you how many women I interviewed for this book who told me outright that money is not important. Just a few days ago, I was speaking with an entrepreneur who told me making money is just not her focus. For some women, it's like a badge of honor that says, "I am at a higher station than that low-life money. I am honorable, I am pure, and I don't need to stoop to the level of talking about money. I choose to work hard because I am passionate about what I do, and I would do it even if I made *no* money." Why would anyone want to do that?

It takes courage to say to yourself, and certainly to others, that you want to make money. Why courage? Because money is such an explosive topic that the mere mention of it will bring up decades and even centuries of money-related issues for yourself, your friends, your family, and your social media readers. It carries the burden of our personal and collective experiences of lack and struggle. It is so loaded that it has become "the conversation we just don't talk about because it's not polite."

If you are someone who stands up and shouts, "I want money," you may very well be deemed as a shallow and greedy person. And who wants that? As women, we want to be liked, approved of, and accepted by others. Saying we want money and we love money is definitely not at the top of the list of how to get the approval and likes we all desire. The people who love money are the "money-hungry, greedy, ugly, unethical" people you have read about and seen in the media, and you don't want to be one of those! Money is seen as opportunistic, selfish, and definitely unfeminine—and I know few women who want to be seen in that way.

Women are supposed to say nice things, make people feel good, and not be overly decisive if we want to be liked and approved of. This has been our cultural conditioning for generations. Maybe it has something to do with being thrown out of the cave if we didn't behave or burned at the stake if we were too vocal (which are really good reasons to stay quiet actually!).

Dr. Valerie Rein, psychologist and author of *Patriarchy Stress Disorder: The Invisible Inner Barrier to Women's Happiness and Fulfillment*, noticed that she and many of her female patients suffered from unhappiness. Sure, you could say, *Who doesn't from time to time?* But women suffer more from unhappiness than men do. In working with hundreds of high-achieving women, Dr. Rein discovered the issues they all struggle with are not just personal. They're rooted in the ancestral and collective traumas experienced by women in the patriarchal world for millennia. She describes how this trauma creates an invisible inner prison that holds women back from stepping into the full power of their authentic presence, unbridled joy, and outrageous success, freedom, and fulfillment.

So there! We have a great excuse if we're looking for one! We can blame our tendency to play small on our collective trauma! All kidding aside, somehow, someway, somewhere, we women learned—either through our own personal experience or through those who came before us—that playing the game of life boldly is simply not safe.

MONEY AND SHAME

When we dare to be bold, there can be backlash. I am a people pleaser and I like to be liked—as many of us women do—and I wasn't prepared for what happened when my husband, Heinz, had dinner with his friend Michael.

They were having dinner at their favorite pizza restaurant when Michael (a sincerely good person) told Heinz he didn't know if he should bring something up about what he read in one of my Facebook posts. I had written a piece about the importance of making money for myself, and I included my yearly business revenue. Michael said he was hesitant to bring it up, but what he read kind of disturbed him. He told Heinz he was a bit shocked about what I wrote. He said he had never seen me as "that kind of person"—the kind who is all about money and publicly states their revenue numbers for all to see.

The truth is, it took me eons to publicly state my earnings. I was also uncomfortable for others to know what my business revenues were because I was scared about what "they" would think of me.

A year earlier, I had posted my yearly revenue in a private Facebook group for entrepreneurs where we were all encouraged to share our annual sales. However, to my horror, I realized I had posted my sales figures to my personal Facebook page for all my friends and family to see. OMG! I was so embarrassed and ashamed and quickly took the post down but not fast enough, as one friend had already commented, "Congratulations, Leslie." I quickly private messaged him and made him promise me he wouldn't tell anyone (sorry, Sammy).

Why? Because I was scared people would look at me differently, just like Michael did when he read that post.

Why are we so ashamed and shamed by others when we say we want money or state what we want to earn? The answers are emotionally, psychologically, and socioculturally complex. There are multiple answers and *many* reasons. I am asking you to reflect on your reasons because those reasons are why you are now making what you do, or more to the point, the reasons you are not making what you want!

Having open conversations with others about what you want to earn can be risky, such as the conversation I had at a particularly memorable workshop I attended. I was a member of a small mastermind group of entrepreneurs who sold physical products on Amazon. We decided we would all meet in person in Seattle, where the consultant who ran our group lived. We were excited to come together to share our common e-commerce and Amazon issues, especially because we had only met virtually during our weekly online meetings. Being an entrepreneur can be lonely as you spend so much time on your own, so we were happy to be together in the same room.

We were a small group of eight people, and the workshop leader asked us to go around the room and share our business goals. People spoke about yearly sales revenue goals, ideas on bringing in new product lines, and the desire to build a business they are proud of. When my turn came, I said, "My goal is to build wealth, and I wanted to earn $20,000 a month after taxes." That was the year I decided to get honest about wanting to earn money, and I seized the moment to announce it—to state it unequivocally and be proud of it.

A few months later, Susan, one of the eight attendees in the workshop and an inspiring person who had become a friend, confided that she had been uncomfortable and astounded with what I had disclosed. She told me she couldn't believe I had actually said it out loud! Years later, she brought it up again, saying how she had never forgotten that moment and she was secretly impressed with my audacity. But even with Susan cheering me on, I'm living proof of just how loaded money is and how we can be perceived negatively for openly talking about it.

Brooke Castillo is a super coach. That is what I call coaches who make mega bucks. She has been forthright about her business practices and structure, and at the time of this writing she does $50 million a year in revenue and openly shares that. One of her goals is to help women make more money and remove the stigma around money. I was excited when I discovered an episode on her podcast, *The Life Coach School*, called "Women and Money." It's episode #324, and I encourage you to listen to it because it's *very* eye-opening.

In the episode, Brooke shares some of the comments and emails she had recently received from women in her coaching program and from people who simply listen to her podcast.

> *"I love your work, but can you please stop talking about money all the time?"*

> *"Why do you have to talk about how much you make; it is distasteful. Stop doing it!"*

"Please stop telling women they can make a million dollars. It is not realistic or possible for them, and you're putting things in women's minds that will be disappointing for them later."

Brooke shares these comments to show how loaded money is, especially for women. There are so many rights and wrongs—so many unspoken rules about who you can talk to about money, what you can say, how you can phrase it. And if you are a woman, you damn well better keep it all a bit quiet, otherwise people will no longer see you as the sweet, feminine woman you want to be seen as.

These rules are a part of why so many women don't make the kind of money they would like to be making. For men, it is expected that money will be their primary focus. For women, we're also accountable for home and family, generally speaking. This can create a conflict most of us deeply understand. Even if a woman does not have children—and I am one of them—stepping out of a dependent role is not always comfortable or easy. It's much more comfortable to be where we are, not pushing ourselves too much and not upsetting the status quo.

If you're a woman who is accustomed to being protected and funded by a wealthy man—a father, husband, or partner—becoming financially empowered can be uniquely challenging.

THE PRINCESS IN THE TOWER SYNDROME

As soon as your eyes landed on the words "princess in the tower," most likely your mind presented you with a picture from a Disney movie where a beautiful princess in a castle is standing at her window and looking out for Prince Charming to come and save her. Let's be honest—that's not so bad! I mean, come on: having some gorgeous, loving, rich guy come and rescue you and take care of you and ensure that you live happily ever after is kind of a nice scenario.

I remember working in New York City in a public relations job I didn't like and at times daydreaming of being saved by my prince. During those hot summer days when I was commuting by subway and inhaling those particular smells only New York subways have (especially in the summer), I would much rather have been in the Hamptons, the exclusive beach towns just a few hours north of the city. There, in my own glorious beach house, I envisioned myself preparing watermelon and feta salad while my husband commuted on Friday nights to see me for the weekend!

I grew up this way, amid these kinds of dreams and social norms, and maybe a few of you did too. Men took care of their wives and the wives took care of them and the children. Regardless of which partner embraces the different roles, there is something naturally beautiful about this design. One partner earns and the other takes care of the home. They both play their parts. Ideally, a harmonious support structure is what a partnership and family should be about. But, as we all know, it doesn't always work out this way. Divorce happens, illness happens, financial troubles happen, death happens, all putting a woman's security at risk. True, this dependent role does work out for some women, but it is a dangerous gamble.

It certainly didn't work for Barbara Huson, author of several bestselling books on women and money, including *Sacred Suc-*

cess: *A Course in Financial Miracles, Overcoming Underearning,* and *Prince Charming Isn't Coming: How Women Get Smart about Money.* Central to Barbara's story is how she handed the millions she inherited from her father over to her husband and watched it all disappear when he ran away with it, lost it, and left her with a million-dollar tax bill.

There are still far too many married women who have no idea about their shared finances because their husbands are "taking care of it." There are countless women, millions actually, who marry "wealthy" men and then proceed to dissociate from "their" money. They live in nice houses, have credit cards for their own purchases, and their partners pay the bills and handle investments. But they, themselves, do not actually "have" the money, nor do they know how to access it.

The point is, marrying a rich man doesn't guarantee a woman will feel rich or even secure. She often has no way to get her hands on the money. She is given credit cards and a budget, but she does not know bank account numbers, how much money is in the retirement accounts, where the investments lay, or how to obtain any of this information. She is out of the loop of her husband's money and yet from the outside is seen as "wealthy"—driving luxurious cars, living in posh homes but secretly feeling she has no security or control of her own life.

The princess in the tower syndrome can happen to women in many different ways. For example, recently a friend's husband was diagnosed with a life-threatening illness. Not only was she in extreme pain, shock, and distress over this awful situation, but she was also gripped by fear as she realized that if he died, she was completely in the dark about their financial standing.

She had no idea where the money was, how to access it, how much she had to live on, or if she was going to be destitute or wealthy if he lost his life. That was a wake-up call for her, and thankfully she has since taken control of their finances.

This is not an unusual situation. Many women accept the traditional roles of wife and mother while men assume the roles of working, making money, and taking care of the money for the family. Not all men are involved in the day-to-day of taking care of the kids and not all women are involved in the day-to-day care of the money and investments. But again, the trouble with this design is how it puts a woman in an insecure and vulnerable position. If life doesn't turn out how she hopes and divorce happens, or if catastrophic illness or death sadly comes, it could wipe out her financial security. This is a scary position for any woman to be in. Does it work out for some women who are not involved in the finances? Sometimes, yes. But suppose you are in the other group?

The truth is, many of the women I know who are now in midlife and who chose not to work and be homemakers have suffered in some ways due to not having their own money, like another friend named Marianne. Before meeting her husband, Marianne, who is now in her fifties, had a high-paying job in finance, but after getting married and having her three children, she decided to stay at home as her husband earned quite a lot of money.

It was a cold day in Chicago, and as we sat on her beautiful couch in her penthouse, Marianne described the misery in her marriage and her desire to split. But she had no money except what her husband gave her to run the house and pay for the groceries, dry cleaning, and other daily living expenses for the family. Her husband paid her credit card bills, but she did not know where the money was or how to access it. Looking out the window and away from me, she told me she was in the process of skimming off some of the money so she could hide it from her husband.

Marianne was paralyzed with fear. She wanted to leave but was scared of what she would lose. All of this gnawing fear was having complex repercussions, not only leaving her feeling like a disempowered princess but now reducing her to skimming the money. Marianne was a super-smart, talented woman, but without some economic control, she lost much of her inner strength and power. She literally did not feel she was in control of her life. All of this chipped away at the integrity, dignity, and grace that were Marianne's true nature.

Fran is another woman who felt caught in a financial web. She is one of thousands of expatriate wives who accompany their spouses around the globe. It's common for global companies to send their executives where needed for short amounts of time—two years to Moscow, then on to London for a year, and then to Zurich—and the spouses and children follow. I have met many of these women when living in Zurich, Switzerland, to be with my Swiss husband. Even though it first sounds quite glamorous to have a life like this, it does take a toll on the trailing spouse's own life. As you can imagine, it's hard to start and keep a job when you may need to leave it at any time.

Fran and I are old friends. We met at a café and ordered cappuccinos. She confessed she was not only unhappy with this lifestyle, which she had been a part of for over twenty years, but she was also unhappy with her husband. She did not mince words: the marriage was bad. She had grown kids living in Miami and she wanted to live near them, but she didn't have the money to do so and knew her husband was not just going to buy her an apartment there along the beach so she could leave. She, too, was in her fifties, wanted to leave her husband but was afraid of what it would mean to her life financially.

I was also a princess in the tower as I explained in Chapter 1. It is typical (even *normal?*) for a woman to be taken care of and supported by her partner financially. Perhaps as you've read these stories, you've recognized yourself in them. Maybe certain stories have stirred up feelings of sadness, worry, defensiveness, or self-righteous anger. I get it, I really do. My primary reason for sharing these stories of struggle is my hope that they bring consciousness and awareness of the risk of what can happen when women put themselves in vulnerable situations. Even more specifically, I want *you* to be in a strong, secure, and independent situation!

INDEPENDENCE IS FREEDOM

What happens when you don't *need* someone else to give you money? Who are you when you no longer need a man, a husband, a partner, a parent, a father, or whoever you depend on? Author Barbara Stanny says being successful, standing in our power, and not depending on someone else to take care of us is our greatest fear.

By standing on our own feet and knowing we can truly take care of our families and ourselves, we truly grow up and take 100 percent responsibility for our money, our relationships, our homes, our jobs, our businesses, and our happiness. We no longer cover up our light and power or hide our dreams and desires in order to remain safe and comfortable. The hard truth is that many of us are afraid of our own power because becoming powerful means we can't act like little girls any longer, we can't hide from our true wants, and we can't pretend we don't know things.

I went kicking and screaming toward becoming a grown-up woman who takes full responsibility for my life, my wealth, and my freedom. I had feelings of privilege that sounded like this:

I deserve to be given _____ *(fill in the blank).*

It's my husband's job to make the big bucks.

I don't want to lose the freedom of living how I want.

I don't want to work that hard.

I am a spiritual person; I don't want to focus on money.

These were some of the disempowering thoughts in my head. But now that I am on this side of success, I realize they were all based on fears of not wanting to stand on my own feet. Suppose I fell or couldn't do it in the first place?

Upon reflection, I realized this was simply a result of the way I grew up. In my family, the men made the big bucks. The women could too, if they chose, but the bottom line was that it was more important you had a guy who made the real money.

When I was twenty-five and newly married to my first husband,

I remember saying to him, "Promise me you will make over $100,000 a year. *Promise me.*" What is most startling to me now about this is that I didn't even think of asking *myself* to make $100,000 a year. It never occurred to me.

Another strong money memory I have comes from when I was sixteen. My mom told me when I get married, I should keep some money to the side so that I always have access to it, just in case. The fact that I remember this so vividly proves what a pivotal moment it was. I knew my mom was transferring to me a piece of sacred woman's knowledge. But why in the world wasn't I taught to make my own money so I wouldn't have to "keep it on the side," which was code for hiding it? It took a long time for me to figure this out.

As I hit my fifties, something in me started to feel not so right, not so honest, and I no longer wanted to sit in my princess tower and wait for someone else to hand me the keys to a prosperous and empowered life. I simply couldn't live with myself anymore because I knew I could be doing much better.

Now it's your turn to reflect on your own money story. Grab a journal or open a document and respond to the questions below. It is normal to feel a range of emotions when you do this because money is such a loaded topic. But the more you excavate the attitudes and memories you have around money, the more you will free yourself from their influence. Sometimes just giving voice to them or writing about them without trying to resolve anything can have a positive effect.

- What beliefs about money were you taught growing up that you made your own?
- How much money do you want to make in your business or profession?
- How does it make you feel to say, "I want and love money!"?
- How would you feel if you became super successful and made a lot of money?

Well done! I know this can push a lot of buttons, and I applaud you for your courage.

QUICK REVIEW

Let's look at where you are now. You have written your authentic success statement and you know what freedom means to you. You also understand that you are in the money-making business, and this is great news because you want money and you love it! Fantastic, you are doing great!

If you are not quite there yet, if you don't have the clarity you're seeking, that's okay too. It will come. And inspiration will come. I know this because I understand the life-giving power that's released when women break through old taboos and dismantle outmoded beliefs about freedom and money in their own lives. In placing your attention in this direction, you have already begun to lay a new foundation for building a truly successful business and greater wealth.

WHERE WE'RE GOING NEXT

In Chapter 1, I shared with you the moment I realized I was not going to wake up on my next birthday in the same financial situation I was currently in—there was just NO WAY. I needed something to change. I needed to step into my power. Although I didn't consciously know it then, that moment was the birth of Key #1. Read on to find out what that is!

Chapter 4

KEY #1: REALLY WANT IT

"Success follows doing what you want to do. There is no other way to be successful."
—Malcolm Forbes

Wanting is powerful. When wanting becomes a burning desire, it gives you the fuel to make that desire a reality. I remember the exact moment my wanting led me to becoming an entrepreneur. It all started with *not wanting* to get a job.

When I was thirty-three, I traveled for seven exciting months throughout Indonesia—something I had always wanted to do. Something about seeing those groups of islands on the map—the Indonesian Archipelago—drew me there. But, as with all good things, after those months of travel and adventure, I knew I had to go back home and face the fact that I needed to get a job.

With wonderful memories of traveling etched into my mind

and heart, I returned to my New York City rent-stabilized rail-road apartment. These quirky apartments were the tenements many immigrants used to live in when they came to the United States. There are no connecting hallways inside the apartments; you simply walk through each little room to get to the next, much like a train car. The crowning glory in my apartment was the bathtub in the kitchen at the end! The whole place had a lot of character.

One morning, I was sitting on my bed with the *New York Times* job section open because in the '90s, that is how you looked for a job. There was no "online" at that time. As I looked through the pages of the Help Wanted ads, reading job title after job title, there was not one single position I wanted in the whole newspaper: Nothing, nada. No.

The whole idea of getting a job in an office—getting up early, putting on pantyhose, commuting on the bus or subway, walking into a huge skyscraper, taking an elevator up, and spending the entire day there—was horrific to me. I hated the idea of losing my freedom.

Leaning back against the pillows on my bed, I had a sudden thought. I remembered the cute children's batik clothing I had seen in Bali just weeks before. I wondered, *If I go back to Bali, and if I buy clothing and bring it back to New York and sell it at a street fair, would I sell any?*

This is a great example of just how powerful *simply wondering* can be. That one little *wonder* was the seed that set me on the path to where I am now with my successful business. Just wondering about possibilities for the business you now have, or the one you will create, can ignite the creation process. Pay close attention when your internal dialogue starts with phrases like:

I wonder if there's a need for...?

What if I were to...?

What would happen if I...?

I wonder...?

When my moment of wonder hit, I took out my calculator and started to punch in numbers: how much it would cost to return to Bali, how much the clothing would cost, how much street fair registration would cost, and how much I thought I could sell the clothing for. I realized that unless the clothing was stolen somewhere along the way, there was no way I could *not* make money doing this.

Back then, there were opportunities to get almost free airline tickets by working as a courier, delivering a package to some unknown person in the arrival airport (can you imagine doing that today?). I had to be thrifty at this stage, when my "wonderings" were just little buds waiting to sprout, so I did it. I got a courier flight, went back to Bali, walked the streets in that stifling heat (I don't know a hotter place in the world than Bali), went to dozens of stores, met with owners, and bought and bought and bought.

I returned to New York full of excitement, with a huge duffel bag of colorful, fun children's clothing. Within just a few days, I got a license to sell at street fairs, bought a folding table, schlepped all the clothing and the table in a taxi to the fair, and set up my table. Before I could finish setting up and displaying the goods, women mobbed my table. This multihued, adorable children's clothing was different. It was original, bright, and breezy, and they had never seen anything like it before. They were literally grabbing items as fast as they could.

Before that day, I had absolutely no sales experience. Zero. But luckily, my mom did. She was at my side the whole day and helped me manage the throng of buyers. At the end of the day—and I will never forget it—I had $800 cash in my hand. I felt so exhilarated that people loved the clothing! Within two weeks, I was sold out of everything I had purchased, jumped back on a plane to Bali, bought more clothing, came back to New York City—and that is how Back from Bali was born.

It didn't happen because I wanted to be a children's clothing purveyor or designer. It didn't happen because I had dreamed of "crushing it" in the world of street fairs. It didn't even happen because I wanted to start a business. It all came to fruition because I really *did not want* to work for someone else in a job where I would have to work the hours they told me to work, take the vacation days they allowed me to take, feel guilty if I needed to call in sick, and wait months or years for the promotion they might want to give me. I *wanted* freedom.

THE POWER OF WANTING

When Elizabeth Gilbert was on *Oprah* following the extraordinary success of her bestselling book, *Eat, Pray, Love*, I'll never forget what she said when asked about her thoughts on how to be successful. Elizabeth answered, "You have to know what you really, really, really want." She stressed that you have to say *really* three times—that was the most important part.

I now know what she meant. In order to create what you want, you have to want it in a way where you simply can't live with yourself if you don't have it. It can't be the kind of wanting that says, *Yeah, I would like it, but I don't want to work that hard*, or, *I would like it, but I also want to do other things.* That kind of wanting doesn't get you very far.

You have to want it as if *not* having it is no longer an option; it's not even a concept that exists in your mind. It has to become a non-negotiable wanting. That is the kind of wanting you need to have in order to step into whatever it is you deeply desire and simultaneously navigate the changes it will ask of you. That is the kind of wanting that got me to where I am now, and it is the kind of wanting that will get *you* to where you want to be.

Without that passion behind your actions, not much is going to happen. It is one of the reasons businesses fail and why my business was just paying for some nice vacations for a while. On *Shark Tank*, the TV program where entrepreneurs pitch their business ideas to the shark investors, it's sometimes the entrepreneurs who don't yet have even one sale who convince one of the sharks to invest in them. It typically comes down to the entrepreneur's strong desire for success or their raw passion for selling their new product. The sharks have that *instinct.* They know that if you invest in someone who really, really, really wants it with all their heart—who has a burning desire—that person will do whatever it takes to get there. When this kind of passion meets with persistence, look out!

Along my entrepreneurial journey, before the success I have now, a turning point came when I realized I wasn't clear enough about what I wanted. My burning desire had dwindled to a flicker. I had allowed myself to linger too long in a state of vagueness, indecision, and wavering, which resulted in a mediocre business for a period of time. I simply wasn't in touch with what I really wanted; I wasn't being honest enough with myself. Therefore, there simply was not enough gas in my tank to get liftoff and make things soar.

Another problem is that I kept changing my mind and putting conditions on what I wanted. I wanted more money, but I didn't want to work that hard. I wanted more success in my business, but I didn't want it to take away time from my spiritual life and the retreats I wanted to attend. I wanted independence and to feel and own my power, but I wanted my dad to buy me clothes (even in my early fifties, I'm embarrassed to say).

Can you relate to any of these requirements and demands?

Do you sense how scattering your focus and priorities impacts your ability to move forward effectively? My wanting was all over the place. It's not possible to have the power you need if one thing you want cancels out the other. It's like pressing on the gas pedal and brake at the same time—you don't go anywhere and you lose a lot of energy.

This is why Elizabeth Gilbert said you must say what you really want three times. By declaring it three times, you are confirming it is the one thing you really want.

I know it is hard to pick just one thing to want. I mean, don't you want many things? I did. I wanted a great relationship, I wanted to have more money, I wanted a better wardrobe, I wanted a more fit body, I wanted to travel, I wanted to get direct guidance from my higher self, I wanted to help animals. The list can go on and on and on and on. How do you choose the one thing out of the many that you want? How do you get to the "really, really, really" part and provide the answer that will change your business and your life?

It is not easy to know what we want. Just think of the mental stew we've had bubbling away on the back burner. The recipe consists of years of conditioning from our parents and families, a big dollop of shared societal values, a generous sprinkling of questionable social media messaging, all added to centuries of attitudes and beliefs about how women should be and what they should want. We have many voices inside of us, directing our lives and choices, that are not our own. This is why we can't hear the guidance from deep within that knows precisely what we want. (But don't worry! Together, we're going to open up the space for you to hear your truest inner voice when we come to Key #7: Embrace Non-Doing.)

Hearing that guidance, getting clear on our wants and our burning desires, takes work and honesty. It means committing to reflecting on ourselves so that we can truly hear what is important to us. Karen, a good friend of mine, told me a dream she once had where a wise feminine being said to her, "It's no wonder that you can't hear yourself given the family that you were born into. Their needs always came first." Without doing the work to know ourselves, we can go through a whole lifetime living someone else's wants and needs. But the potential of that happening to you can stop right here and now.

I have a fabulous "secret" to share with you that will help you drop even deeper into the pool of your wants and desires.

YOUR YEARNING IS YOUR KEY

Dr. Claire Zammit, founder of Feminine Power, the women's transformation program, is a remarkable teacher you'll be reading more about in the chapters to come. Her company, Evolving Wisdom, has ranked at #83 on *Inc.* magazine's list of the top 5,000 fastest-growing private companies in the United States, and it has generated over $50 million in revenue, reaching millions of women from more than 180 countries. As a heavy hitter in the personal development field and one of my primary mentors, Dr. Zammit always gets to the essential truths. She says the question to ask yourself when you are trying to figure out what your big want is, What do I *yearn* for?

Yearning is the real truth behind wanting because it's sourced from a far deeper place. Your yearning is closer to your soul than wanting alone is. It is the seed inside of you that is bursting to break through the soil and reach the light of day. This soul seed talks to you through the beautiful ache that we know as a yearning. It is your *entelechy.* Entelechy, a word I learned from Dr. Zammit, is now one of my favorite words because it is evocative and powerful. It is an ancient Greek word that Aristotle spoke of that means "the realization of potential." The entelechy of the oak seed is to become an oak tree; the entelechy of you is to become your greatest self. Don't you just love that? Your yearning is the insistence of your soul that your unique gifts be fully realized and shared generously with the world around you.

Ask yourself right now, what do you yearn for?

Doesn't it feel good to ask yourself this question? In addition to bringing you closer to your soul, another reason this question likely feels good is because what you yearn for is coming from your true values and authenticity. It's deeper than material things or different circumstances. I'll give you some examples:

- You want a new car, but perhaps your yearning is to feel more valued.
- You want to lose weight, but perhaps your yearning is to be loved.
- You want a divorce and to move house and home, but perhaps your underlying yearning is for more self-care and time just for you.
- You want to make more money, but you really yearn to feel empowered and independent.

What I've learned is that those yearnings inside of you—such as the yearning to be the go-to person in your industry because you're firing on all cylinders and people see it, the yearning to earn the kind of money that will allow you to give in a variety of ways, the yearning to thrive and enjoy life to the maximum, and the yearning to step into the highest version of yourself—are your most precious allies and will help you get there. Those urgent feelings inside of you are messages for you to *do* something. They are shouting, *Listen to me!*

THE MARRIAGE OF WANTING, DESIRING, AND YEARNING

Not everyone's yearnings, wants, and desires are the same, of course. I definitely don't want to go bungee jumping or climb 14,000-foot mountains, but some women do—you brave women! I have a good friend who is a photographer, and she literally hangs out of open planes so she can capture the full gloriousness of mountain ranges. I definitely don't want to do that, but I'm glad she does, as her photos are breathtaking.

The yearning and wanting inside of you is there because it speaks of something important you need to do or express. It wouldn't be inside of you if it weren't meant to come out. You wouldn't be reading this book if you didn't deeply desire to be a successful entrepreneur. Not every woman wants to have her own business. *You wouldn't have the desire to build your business so that you can have a life of freedom if you were not meant to do this.* Instead, you might have another desire in you, such as training horses, or stopping sex trafficking, or being a professional athlete or a professor of geology. There is a self-directed path calling you. Heeding the call—answering it with your attention and care—is one of the most transformative and rewarding things you will ever do.

I told you the story of what I really wanted, which was to make more money. But that was only one part of the story, albeit an essential one because it allowed me to go to the next level of understanding myself. The greater truth is that my yearning extends beyond money. I could have become a stockbroker, a day trader, or a pharmaceutical executive if money was my primary goal. My wanting for money and autonomy was the bridge to my yearning to stand in my power, to feel in control of my life, and to be able to live the freedom that feels right in my very soul. The money is a by-product of me going after my yearning, going after what I really, really, really wanted, which was total empowerment and the ability to live my greatest life and not have anything hold it back, including lack of money.

When you get in touch with what you really want, what you yearn for, and what your burning desire is, you get to the fire that will ignite your businesses and life. And you want to get to your fire because you are going to need it to carry you along.

The moment I was unflinchingly honest with myself—when I admitted *I want money and I love money* and had the courage to say it to myself out loud—was the moment things started to change and flow toward the success I now have. This is what I want you to have too.

So let's go there.

GIVE YOURSELF PERMISSION TO BE HONEST

Getting clear about what we want goes hand in hand with being honest with ourselves about what we want. Yet, we often have a hard time being honest with ourselves about such important matters. One of the biggest reasons comes down to the "j-word"—judgment. Even if we easily identify what we "really, really, really want," we often have judgments about it. Then we're prone to sabotaging our success because we judge our want. We do this by thinking things like:

It's not helpful enough.

I'm being too selfish.

It's too materialistic.

Who am I anyway to want that?

I'm getting too big for my britches.

What will people think?

What will my family think?

It will take too much time.

And on and on.

Can you relate to this? All of these anxious concerns can stop us from saying yes to our deepest want. But if you want the authentic success you defined for yourself, if you want the big bucks, and if you want to live your freedom, you have to start by giving yourself *permission* to say what it is you really, really, really want.

Breathe that in for a moment.

Give yourself permission to admit to yourself what it is you really want. Let go of whether it seems selfish or egotistical, or whatever judgment you are putting on it, and just say it. When you give yourself permission to be authentic with yourself, you release years (maybe even decades) of attitudes, beliefs, thoughts, and feelings that no longer serve you.

I remember well the moment that changed everything for me, the moment in my little office when I drew a deep line in the sand and proclaimed that there was no way I was going to spend another birthday not making over $100,000 a year—no way. I decided there would be no more wishy-washy wants for me. I was going all-in! I was going for what was, for me, the want of all wants. I decided to make the success of Back from Bali my big want. As I came to understand over time, this wanting was supercharged by an even greater *yearning* for freedom.

In that moment, I literally felt something restricting leave my body, and if that something could have talked it would have said, *Whoo-hoo! What took you so long?*

You don't need to wait as long as I did. I was in my mid-fifties when I finally gave voice to that want. If you find yourself still dragging your feet, I'm going to help you kick-start your next level of success by giving you permission right now to declare to yourself what you really want. Say it out loud! And say it proud!

I really, really, really want _____.

USE YOUR FEMININE POWER TO CREATE

When you combine your wanting and deepest yearning with action, you ignite your feminine power. It is feminine power because the wanting is coming from an authentic place deep inside of you. It is not coming from what you think success is or a need to impress your Facebook friends and fans with enviable posts. It is not coming from a need to gain approval from your family, colleagues, or closest friends. It is coming from the heart of you—from what is most meaningful to you. Therefore, the action that ensues is in alignment with your deepest values, principles, and ideals. I can tell you from my own experience that this kind of aligned action is so nourishing to the seed of greatness within you—your entelechy—that at a certain point, the next evolution of yourself can no longer wait. This is your rising! And whether you are thirty-five or sixty-five, this is the rising of you as a woman entrepreneur and feminine powerhouse.

One of the primary differences between masculine power and feminine power is that the former takes a linear approach, using step-by-step processes to achieve goals. Thank goodness that approach exists. We can look at the sales funnel that is a cornerstone of online digital marketing as an example of a masculine creation. Sales funnels are the epitome of a step-by-step process, turning cold leads into warm leads and then into sales. And yep, this marketing map was, indeed, first developed by a man by the name of Elias St. Elmo Lewis, an American advertising pioneer, in 1898.

The feminine approach is different. When it comes to sales and marketing, feminine power is about building relationships and taking the time to find out what matters most to her customers or clients. When it comes to your entrepreneurial rising, the feminine approach is about tapping into your yearning, calling on your intuition, and asking you to be 100 percent honest about what authentic success is to you. It is about making a conscious decision to allow yourself to want it. And believe me, dear sisters, that is powerful—so powerful it can create multimillion-dollar businesses without funnels!

Powerful, intentional wanting is important because once you claim it, magic starts to happen. Magic is just what you want when you're opening the door to more success, more money, and more freedom. You want to produce your desired effect—the realization of your dream—with ease and enchantment. I just know you do! Remember, in my case I had that strong wanting when I was thirty-three years old to *not* get a job that propelled me to start my business. Twenty years later, my strong wanting to make real money and be highly successful brought me to the multiple seven-figure business I now have. It is the power of that wanting that is going to give you your success. And it is the force that is going to lift you up and keep you going through the tough times and doubts that go with the territory.

We women sometimes make the mistake of only focusing on what the business is going to do and *how* we are going to do it. Sure, the how is also important. But before you get into the action steps of doing, you need to get in touch with what you feel, especially the feelings associated with your wanting. Just tap into your wanting for a moment. Sense it. Feel it moving through you. It is the thing inside of you that is bursting to get what it really wants. Go ahead, say yes to it!

YOUR POWER IS YOUR WANTING

You are reading this book to learn how to have a successful business. I know you are looking for me to tell you exactly *how* to do it and not to offer generalized fluff. This is why Key #1 is Really Want It. Starting with a strong wanting is more important than the things you might think are essential for your business such as a website, or social media following, or even finding your first product or service to sell. If you're just now taking those first steps, all of that will come, but it will all be exponentially more effective when you get clear on the wanting and burning desire.

Kelly, a mom of three boys who lives in Denver, started a business offering an after-school sports program. During our preliminary mentoring session, she told me many of her ideas about the kinds of programs she wanted to offer. But when I asked her to tell me about her burning desire, she said she wasn't sure. She didn't feel a strong wanting; she just "kind of wanted to earn some extra money." Even though that is a perfectly respectable desire, it is *not* an entrepreneurial-level desire. That's called having a hobby. And you, beautiful woman, want to be a successful entrepreneur, like my friend Sonya.

Sonya had such a burning desire to transform people's lives through teaching meditation that she was able to go from bankruptcy to a multimillion-dollar business in a couple of years. I know her personally and watched this transformation happen, and I want *you* to know this is really possible when your wanting is that strong. Sonya was able to do this because of the multiple roaring flames of her burning desire:

- To get out of her painful financial situation.
- To bring inner peace to as many people as she can across the globe.
- To embody the greatness she always knew was inside of her.

Now, that is feminine power! Strong wanting can and does create miracles.

Think about a time in your life when you really wanted something and achieved it. I bet your wanting was very strong. And that is the kind of wanting you need to have for your business now—whether you've already launched it or are in the beginning stage of formulating your business idea. Again, when you have that strong wanting, your business will explode. Breathe some life into your burning desire and you *will* have it.

In order to get crystal clear about what you want, answer these four questions:

- What do you really, really, really want?
- Beneath your wanting, what do you yearn for? Is it recognition? Creative expression? To be of service? Something else?
- Why do you want your business?
- Are you willing to give yourself permission to want what you want?

QUICK REVIEW

You know what your authentic success and freedom mean to you. You are developing a great relationship with money and are getting comfortable saying you *want* it and *love* it and aren't afraid to say so. Great, you have your foundation down! Adding to that, you have just discovered Key #1 and are either abundantly clear about what you want when it comes to your business or are seriously contemplating it.

WHERE WE'RE GOING NEXT

Now it's time to learn Key #2, one of the most powerful concepts in life, which, when implemented into your business, will bring extraordinary success. There is not a single successful person who ever existed who didn't apply this. Turn the page to find out what it is.

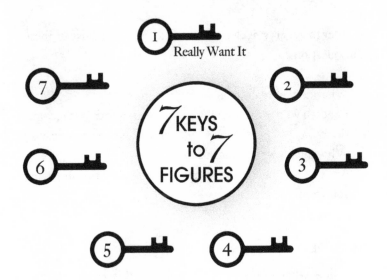

Really Want It

7 KEYS to 7 FIGURES

ᴄ﹂ *Chapter 5* *ᴐ﹍*

KEY #2: FOCUS ON IT

*"Most people have no idea of the giant capacity we
can immediately command when we focus all of our
resources on mastering a single area of our lives."*
—Tony Robbins

Sitting in my little office in the depths of my disappointment in myself, I felt as far away as I could be from success. But how could this be? I was running two businesses I loved. In addition to Back from Bali, there was Girl Power, a mind-body-spirit program I designed for girls ages seven to thirteen. It was a natural outgrowth of my education as a clinical social worker and many years in the field of transformational psychology. I had a deep yearning to do work that was meaningful and empowering and that focused specifically on body image, healthy eating, positive mindset, and self-love for young girls during those formative and vulnerable years. Although my work today has shifted to mentoring women entrepreneurs, I've always had a passion for uplifting the feminine at every age and stage of life, and Girl Power soothed my soul.

At that time, it may have looked to the outside world like I was doing very well, but I knew better. The truth was that neither of the businesses produced the kind of money or achievement I was yearning for. Both businesses did okay; they paid the bills and gave us a nice travel fund for vacations. And although both businesses were based on values that were dear to my heart, both also fell short of giving me the freedom, independence, and income I truly desired.

As I sat in my office, simmering with the yearning to do better, I had a huge realization. It was one of those lightbulb moments people talk about that literally changed the course of my life. I realized the reason I hadn't yet reached the success I was capable of was because I wasn't *focused*. My attention and energy were split, veering off in multiple directions.

For seven years, I managed to juggle both businesses at the same time. I created Girl Power during an exciting period when I had just moved to Zurich to be with my soon-to-be husband. I was overjoyed to be starting this new chapter of my life and ran groups for girls all over Switzerland, traveling to different schools with my box of supplies, pillows to sit on, and bags of popcorn to eat. I also ran a workshop for moms called Raising Healthy Daughters.

When I wasn't leading a training or workshop, I was planning the colors and patterns for the next clothing collection, communicating with my manufacturers in Bali, and keeping up with the bookkeeping and finances. There was a lot of multitasking required in order to get everything done, as you can imagine.

No matter how passionate I was about the work I was doing,

this style and pacing of running my businesses, I ultimately discovered, wasn't going to be sustainable.

UP AND DOWN AND DOWN AND UP

Remember what it was like when you were a kid, sitting on one end of a seesaw, probably holding on with a mighty grip while your friend sat on the opposite end. If all went well, when you gently floated up, she would go down, then vice versa. Up and down, up and down. It was fun, right?

This was the image that came to me on that day in my office. The trouble, I realized, was that my two businesses were two ends of a seesaw. When I focused on one of the businesses, it would start to go up—positive reviews would rise, new inquiries would flow in, revenues would increase. But the opposite would occur with the other business. When my focus was on Back from Bali—sourcing new fabrics and designs and implementing marketing strategies—sales would go up. Girl Power, on the other hand, would go down, meaning the cancelation of a workshop or an interested new school deciding the program wasn't in their budget after all. I would stop focusing on Back from Bali and put all my attention on Girl Power again. More girls would join my groups, and I'd receive calls from schools to schedule more classes. Then guess what? Back from Bali would head south.

I realized I did not have the focus nor the bandwidth for both businesses to succeed at the level I was working to achieve. When we are overextended, nothing gets the attention it needs to reach momentum, and all our well-intended efforts can lead to mediocrity or failure.

In my lightbulb moment, I knew that attaining success and money meant I had to let go of one of my businesses, both of which I had worked hard to bring into the world. In many ways, they felt like my children. I had grown them both from infancy, and now it felt as if I had to kill one of them. This was an inner conflict that tormented me to my core. I knew if I didn't choose one, I would have no chance of allowing the full business potential that was lying dormant inside of me to rise. It was one of the most difficult choices because I had birthed both of these businesses from the seeds of inspiration. But I had to stop being a worrier and be a warrior instead. I had to make a choice.

As I weighed my options, I heard the voice of my inner judge speaking to me with a kind of steely certainty. "You should definitely keep Girl Power; it is helpful and spiritual," she said. "You are doing something positive for young girls. You can help and perhaps change the course of a girl's life."

She's right, I thought.

But she had more to say. "Your Back from Bali business is selfish and money-focused. It's just about clothing—so superficial! It isn't really helpful, and it certainly isn't deep. Girl Power is better! Back from Bali is materialistic, and it's just about you!"

Wow, opinionated! As "judgment girl" continued her rant, there was a welling up inside of me that grew stronger and stronger. No matter how loudly judgment girl asserted herself, there was another part of me that was even louder.

Rising from my gut and my heart, I heard the voice of my higher self. Not only did I hear her, but I felt her. She said, "Do the Bali business."

To my surprise, I realized it was my head that was vying for Girl Power, not my heart. My ego wanted me to look good, and it was trying hard to convince me to keep doing things that *seemed* to be more altruistic and positive. But my gut and my heart spoke to me so clearly in that moment—clearer than almost any other time in my life. "Focus on Back from Bali, drop Girl Power" was the unequivocal directive.

I decided in that moment to close down Girl Power and focus 100 percent on my importing business. That was the moment that catapulted me into the success I now have. When I made that decision for real, the signals of affirmation I received were like the kind I'd only read about. I felt chills up and down my spine, and it was as if I could hear angels rejoicing and singing hallelujah. Once I said a wholehearted yes to Back from Bali, it felt as if the universe had been holding its breath for a long time and finally was able to exhale, saying, "What took you so long? Gee whiz, girl!"

Sometimes we have to say no to one thing in order to say yes to something greater. I've also learned no one else can say yes for you—not even your inner wisdom, your higher self. She is there nudging you along, but *you* have to make the choice. This is one of the core reasons I've written this book: to help you to find the courage and clarity to recognize your true yeses and noes.

FOCUS IS ONE OF YOUR SUPERPOWERS

When I made that one huge decision to let go of one business and give my full attention to the other, my life got easier and much happier. A few months into my new one-business reality, I wrote in my journal:

> *I am so happy not running around doing workshops. I feel so happy that I have time to see friends, to be at home, to exercise, or to write. This is my bliss, doing what I want. I feel happy that I don't have to prepare for Girl Power today. I love my life now.*

As my focus on Back from Bali grew, I was no longer feeling overwhelmed by running myself ragged with both businesses. Gone were the days when I would drive all over the countryside to lead the after-school groups at different locations, prepare for and run weekend seminars, market that business, and *then* address all of the needs of my importing business including traveling to Bali.

Listen, I realize this might not sound bad to you, but I was stressed. I was tired. I wanted to hide. I sometimes just wanted to escape altogether. I fantasized about running away to travel full time and just letting everything go. All of my "good work" was draining me, not feeding me.

Then, with one small thought, I released myself from the prison that only I had created. I went from being spread way too thin to ultra-focused.

Key #2 to having more money and freedom is Focus on It because focus is *that* important. You need to be decisive and choose where you really want your focus to be if you want to be successful. Without focus, nothing you do can fully thrive. Have you heard the saying that where your attention goes, energy flows? This speaks to a law in our universe stating that whatever you focus on expands. It works every time. If you'd like to test this out, try it on something simple (and universally loved)—chocolate. Focus on the idea of eating chocolate. First, see it in your mind. Is it a truffle, a candy bar, or perhaps a luscious little bowl of mousse? Recall the aroma of your favorite type of chocolate and imagine biting into and savoring the creamy sweetness inside your mouth. Do all of this, and do it frequently, and at some point, you are going to *want* to eat chocolate and nothing will stop you from getting some. Put your heart and soul and focus into creating a kick-ass successful business, and you will build a successful business.

Is it that simple? Yes, it is.

When you aim your attention at something that matters deeply to you and minimize energy-draining distractions, you are gathering internal forces that are extraordinarily powerful. Focus is one of the keys to building anything, from a skyscraper to an online empire to a painting or a sculpture. Whenever you encounter a woman who is enjoying success in her life, I guarantee she harnesses the power of focus on a consistent basis.

I CAN DO IT ALL!

You can do it all, right? Wrong. You think you can, and you may tell yourself defensively, "But I love all the things I do." Believe me, I know. You are creative, you have many different interests, and you have more to offer the world than "just" your products and services. Again, I understand, and it's true that you have more to offer the world than can be summarized in a few clever paragraphs on your website. But please don't fool yourself any longer and think for one more moment that you can do it all because you can't—at least not all at the same time.

We women are expert multitaskers, and in certain moments, doing more than one thing at a time works out well. We can respond to an urgent client text while rocking a toddler to sleep after having just turned on a slow cooker so the lentil soup is ready by dinnertime. But there is nothing *expert* about the results we get from attempting to work this way on a regular basis. According to *Time* magazine's April 2017 article titled, "Why Multi-tasking Is Bad for You," the neuroscience is clear: we are wired to be mono-taskers. One study found that just 2.5 percent of people are able to multitask effectively. That is a very small percentage. When the rest of us attempt to do two or more complex activities simultaneously, it simply does not work. The quality of the work suffers in small or large ways.

"Okay, I get that," you might say. "We should definitely not text and drive, but shifting focus between different projects or running different businesses is…well, different." Actually, that is not true either. According to the *Time* article, "Switching back and forth from project to project, like a hummingbird darting from flower to flower and then back to the original flower, can impair our ability to function at our finest."

You can attempt to be a part-time artist and a part-time businesswoman, but you may discover that your results are mediocre in both arenas rather than stellar in one. This turned out to be true for me, despite my desires, intentions, and efforts. With all the work I had been doing—private practice therapy sessions, running four to five girls' groups a week, creating and facilitating weekend workshops, working at an outdoor holiday market in the dead of winter selling clothing for five straight weeks (seven days a week), and building my online company selling women's clothing that I had designed—I was earning only $68,000 a year.

I was damn proud of that $68,000, and depending on where you live, that might be enough money for you. But it wasn't the kind of freedom and money I wanted. More to the point, I was exhausted, overwhelmed, and miserable. On the positive side, feeling that way probably allowed me to be more receptive when the insight came that I needed to let one of my business babies go. Yeah, it was scary. But I was too worn down physically and emotionally to put up a fight for what my ego was striving for. Letting go brought a rush of support from the universe, and things began to flow and became easier. When people ask me why I gave up Girl Power, I explain I decided to own *my* own girl power. I decided to be kind to and true to myself, and with that, I was suddenly working fewer hours and making more money.

We're conditioned to believe that our busy-ness *is* our business. And we often feel that if we are working many hours, we are doing all we can be doing. But as we discussed in Chapter 2 and as you will be certain of by the time you finish reading this book, more is not always the answer. Being busy, feeling overwhelmed, and working later and longer than everyone else is not the badge of honor we sometimes hope it will be.

Women love to say, "Look at all I do. I'm Superwoman!"

I say, "Screw the Superwoman badge."

Instead, put on the following badge, and watch your bank account and satisfaction levels grow.

I HONOR MYSELF FOR BEING:

focused,

centered,

grounded,

and

empowered.

WHAT ABOUT BALANCE?

You might be wondering at this point about balance. You might think, "Isn't having a balanced life important? If I focus 100 percent on my business and finances, I'll have no balance. Isn't finding that elusive thing called 'balance' one of the keys to a happy life?"

Let me get right to the point: if you really want money and freedom, you cannot have perfect balance—at least not right now. I invite you to do the radical act of throwing out the conventional idea that our goal is to achieve balance. "Balance," as most of us think of it, is more akin to an inner-peace fantasy we've been marketed and sold. If we do a little bit of this and a little bit of that, then we can achieve balance in our life.

Forget that.

If you take that approach, what you get is mediocrity in all the little bits of this and little bits of that. You will make little bits of money, have little bits of success, and have little bits of freedom. That is not what you want. You want real entrepreneurial success and real freedom, and 100 percent focus is the art and skill that will get you there.

Even if you do achieve something close to balance, it's not going to look the way you expect it to. If you're just starting out as an entrepreneur, it's not going to come immediately. It's going to have to be part of your long-term plan. Yes, you will need to work hard but not all the time. When I made my life-altering decision to go for it, to be successful, to make money, and to focus, I spent months working very hard. For the first few years after making the promise to myself to earn more money, I worked my butt off, which often meant seven days a week and evenings. But looking at the longer view, at how I was working and living over the course of a year, showed a fuller picture, and I made sure I had downtime too. For me, balance looked more like a Picasso than a yin-yang symbol. But at the beginning, I did what we all must do: put 100 percent of ourselves in it with focus and passion.

Susan, one of the entrepreneurs I interviewed for this book, operates a thriving e-commerce business in home decor. She says, "The trouble with many entrepreneurs is they *talk* about wanting a business, but in reality, they just want to have a business on the side that doesn't interfere too much with their life. To be successful, you have to get out of your comfort zone and work long hours, at least at the beginning. You have to go all-in." I totally agree, Susan!

Building a business is like planning a big wedding. You need to work hard because there are so many details to manage—the dress, the venue, the food, the ceremony, the invitations, the guests, the music, the decorations, the setup of the tables and chairs, and *more*. But after it is all over, you and your partner get to go on a honeymoon where you enjoy lots of downtime, including recovering from the wedding. After the honeymoon, hopefully you both go back to work feeling refreshed. My mom and her sister Judy ran a party planning business called Party Artistry, and now my cousin Tracy runs it. If you've never attempted this, you can't fully imagine how much work it takes to make the perfect wedding come true. "Having a balanced life" while in the thick of the planning is not the behavior strategy that will bring that dream wedding to fruition. Some sacrifices have to be made to make sure the work gets done. There will be times—especially when you are at the beginning of building your business or looking to up-level it—when you will need to work a lot but again, *not all the time*. Working all the time is called being a slave, and remember, you are not going to be doing that. You are in the freedom business!

You'll also have to adapt to new demands as your life changes. For example, when you have a newborn baby, it's pretty darn hard in the first few months to keep up your sex life, work out regularly, and focus on your business as well. Balance goes out the window because that baby needs you, and so does your business. Both baby and business are going to eat up all of your time. Babies and weddings and other major life events are the times that require *perspective*—to remember why you're doing what you're doing and to remember the mantra that says, "Yes, I'll work hard *but not all the time.*" As your business grows, you will implement systems and hire help so you'll increasingly be living your freedom and making money.

Alice, who was trying to build a product-based business to sell online, was struggling because she had two very different products she was working on at the same time. One of them was already manufactured but had poor sales, and the other was in the idea stage. At the beginning stages of building a product-based business, you typically have to try many different products and several strategies including manufacturing, packaging, shipping, and marketing strategies. At some point, you need to let go of what is not working and focus on one thing that might. Alice needed to take that decisive step in order to allow her business to thrive, and she did. She made the hard choice and got focused.

Sometimes we have to make tough choices. Mr. Wonderful from *Shark Tank* is well known for advising some entrepreneurs to end their businesses because, as he says it, "It is a cockroach that needs to be squashed." Yes, he is tough, but I admire his focus and honesty because of the results they bring.

Charlotte spent years trying to build her mentoring business while simultaneously producing her own music, painting, and giving her support to her husband who had his own finance business. They were all worthy and creative pursuits that she loved, but all combined, they were not helping her get where she wanted to be with her business. Then her husband, Michael, and his business partner split, and he was out of a job. Just as he was about to begin looking for another job, Charlotte asked Michael to join forces with her to build the mentorship business instead. To those looking in from the outside, this seemed like a crazy idea. Charlotte earned very little money from mentoring, Michael was out of a job, and they had no savings and were in debt. Most people would have opted to at least let Michael get some work and bring in money while she builds the business, but not Charlotte. She said, "We both have to be all-in. We both have to focus only on this one vision." That's when their mentorship business went from near bankruptcy to a multimillion-dollar business in two years. *That* is the power of focus!

Focus is the power needed to ignite your burning desire. When you take all of your wanting and yearning and combine it with focus—*boom!* Now you have the fire to create your success.

With that in mind, ponder these questions:

- On a scale from one to ten—with one being completely unfocused and ten being ultra-focused—how much focus do you have on your business?
- Are you juggling too many professional and/or personal interests now?
- Have you been running around but not getting anywhere?
- Which business or interest needs your attention to thrive?
- Are you ready to make the choices that having focus will require of you?

QUICK REVIEW

You have learned about Key #1, the significance of really wanting it, and you have a burning desire to live your freedom and
make serious money. You are getting comfortable with the idea
of standing up and shouting, "I love money!" Your whole attitude about money and freedom is shifting now. Can you feel it?
You know it's about empowerment and independence. Adding
to that, you have just learned about the power of focus and why
it is one of the master keys to your success, today and into the
brilliant future that is waiting for you.

WHERE WE'RE GOING NEXT

Now it's time to learn Key #3. It's time to get humble, because
you don't know what you don't know. What do I mean? Turn
the page to find out.

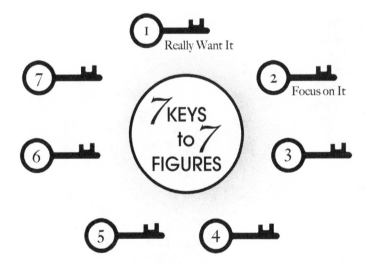

Chapter 6

KEY #3: BECOME A FEROCIOUS LEARNER

"I don't divide the world into the weak and the strong, or the successes and the failures, those who make it or those who don't. I divide the world into learners and non-learners."
—BENJAMIN BARBER

After making the decision to focus on Back from Bali, I made a life-changing step to attend a three-day conference in Seattle for merchants who sell their products on Amazon. After checking into my room, I went down to the lobby restaurant, which was already filled with Amazon sellers talking among themselves. Although there were women present, the great majority of attendees were men. I felt totally out of my depth and yet was excited and thrilled to be part of this. On a scale from one to ten, my understanding of how to sell on Amazon was maybe a 0.5. I knew next to nothing.

As I was surrounded by Amazon seller gods and goddesses, I heard things like this:

"I sell $40,000 a month on Amazon."

"I just sold my Amazon business and am starting a brand-new one."

"I sell 200 units a day."

I felt like a first-grader who was incorrectly put into the sixth grade with all the big kids. There was a whole world out there made of keywords and SEO (search engine optimization), shipping and fulfillment services, and profit and loss statements, all of which were Greek to me. There were speakers talking on topics such as establishing affiliate programs, writing bullet points and titles that sell, setting up for sales tax, developing seller apps to communicate with customers, getting reviews, creating product categories, and building a product feed.

Don't get me started on the product feed. It is a complicated spreadsheet where you enter your product information, and once you upload it into Amazon's system, they magically transform it into the page you see when you go looking for something you want to buy on Amazon (like a swimsuit cover-up or a pair of shoes). In the early stages of my business, that feed was one of the banes of my existence. A low point was when I incorrectly uploaded my German spreadsheet feed, which was supposed to be uploaded to Amazon Germany, into the Amazon US system, automatically changing all my US product listings into the German language. Don't ask!

Anyway, back to the conference.

I would run from one session to another taking massive amounts of notes and wondering if I ever would get to the point of understanding any of this. Yet, I was thrilled to be there because I could feel, hear, and see the vast potential awaiting me.

I went into one of the sessions where an entertaining and dynamic woman speaker was talking about trends and how to choose sellable products. I was mesmerized by her knowledge and her insights. It was as if I stumbled into the Wizard of Oz's back room and was getting a glimpse of how all those levers were working. The curtain was pulled back just enough to see that there was a system behind all of this.

After the speaker finished, I tracked her down in the hallway where she was already surrounded by a group of people wanting her to help them with their businesses. I managed to get one of her cards. It said, Lisa Suttora, Consultant.

Over the next few months, I tried to put into action some of the things I learned at the conference, but I wasn't getting very far. I was doing four to five sales a day online, which was the equivalent of approximately $4,000 a month in revenue. I was thrilled I was doing even that, but after paying for my products, shipping them from Bali to Amazon's warehouse, and then Amazon taking their cut of the sale, plus paying their warehouse and pick-and-pack fees, there wasn't much left for me. This was not the money and freedom I wanted.

One Saturday morning, Heinz and I were getting ready to go to the outdoor farmers market we went to each weekend to buy our vegetables. We were talking about the business, which we always love to do, and he said to me, "Why don't you call that

Lisa person you met at the conference and see if she could help you?" I had already kind of forgotten about Lisa, and Heinz's nudge reminded me of how impressed I was with her. So I did it. I emailed her and asked to set up a call.

I'll never forget our first conversation. I explained to Lisa how I find and bring clothing back from Bali to the United States and sell it on Amazon. Her response was clear and direct: "I would love to help you build your brand." My response was, "What brand?" I didn't think of myself as someone who had a brand. Names like Ralph Lauren or Zara or Lululemon—those are real brands, I thought. I never even considered that I might have a *brand*. It was a totally new concept to me.

Lisa saw something in me I didn't even know was there—she saw I had a brand in the making. I wasn't just selling random products on Amazon like toilet paper, plus phone rechargers, plus vitamins, plus scarves, which many sellers with the goal of getting a sale any way they can do. I have a *niche*, which, in my case, means I specialize in women's warm-weather original clothing from Bali. She saw what I couldn't yet see: I already had something of massive potential value. And it went beyond the value of the products I sold on Amazon; it was also about my own value as an entrepreneur.

Months later, Lisa wrote this to me:

When we first spoke, I was blown away by how much you had going for you as a businesswoman, and yet you didn't see your talent and potential.

After our first call, I made one of the smartest decisions I have ever made for my business and hired Lisa Suttora to be my consultant, thus beginning our working relationship, which continues to this day. When I first hired Lisa, my Amazon revenue was $50,000 a year. After working with her for several months and implementing her teachings, my business doubled in sales to $100,000 by the end of that year. That is a 100 percent increase in a matter of months. Having a mentor to teach me transformed my business.

You see, sometimes we don't even see our own value and the potential of what we already hold in our hands. Sometimes we need an outside perspective that can mirror back to us who we are and what is possible.

WATCH FOR THE NUDGES

It's important to stay awake to the nudges you receive. Sometimes they come from inside of you; sometimes they come from a trusted friend, a loving spouse, or another outside source. Be watchful of the inspiration that comes to you to nudge you toward taking your next steps. Your job is to notice the nudges and take action.

ASKING FOR HELP SHOWS STRENGTH

Beautiful woman, we don't know what we don't know. One of the traits to cultivate in order to be more successful is to be humble and acknowledge that we may need help, that perhaps we can't do it alone, and that there is much more to learn. Indeed, we need to become *ferocious learners*—entrepreneurs who love to learn and do so with a passionate hunger. One of the fastest and best ways to learn is to learn from a seasoned coach, mentor, consultant, or anyone else you hire to help you succeed.

For some, asking for help can feel like a sign of weakness, but I see it as exactly the opposite. It is the strong, intelligent, and open-minded entrepreneur who recognizes that she doesn't know what she doesn't know and looks for a mentor or consultant to guide her.

At another conference for women entrepreneurs I attended, one of the speakers was the extraordinary Ingrid Vanderveldt. Ingrid was the first Entrepreneur in Residence for Dell Technologies, where she created a $100 million credit fund, and is now the founder and CEO of the Empowering a Billion Women movement. She is such an inspiration to me, and her enthusiasm is contagious. Her journey to success has been thrilling, but what impresses me most is her emphasis on how essential the mentor is to growth and success. During her presentation at the conference, she described her process of choosing the mentor who she knew could help her and how she had to convince him that she was worth his time. He put her through many tests before he committed to working with her. What I took away from Ingrid's talk that day changed something in me. I realized it's actually the great ones who know they cannot get to where they want to be without the right guidance from someone who knows how to get them there.

If you have ever thought, "I can do it on my own," I completely understand that thinking. But it may very well take you a much longer time, and you may not get as far as you could if you were guided by a talented coach. Again, it's a quality of strength to allow ourselves to be guided by someone who already knows what we will one day know as well.

THE SCHOOL OF ENTREPRENEURSHIP—A LIFE-CHANGING CURRICULUM

Being an entrepreneur is like being enrolled in a university curriculum that never ends. You never graduate and you never get a diploma because the school of entrepreneurship gives you something else. What you get from the school of entrepreneurship is an incredible education not only in finance, marketing, sales, and operations but in something even *more* valuable than all those combined—you get an education about yourself and your capabilities.

Ultimately, the reason the school of entrepreneurship is life-changing is because of *who you become* in the process of building a business. You learn about yourself in ways you couldn't imagine. While you see your weaknesses, you get to choose to put more attention on your strengths and potential.

As I began to achieve success in my business, it profoundly changed the way I look at myself. Then as now, I am damn proud of what I have achieved. No one handed it to me. I did it myself. Come what may—economic disaster, product failure, having Amazon shut down my product listings (something that actually did happen, temporarily thankfully), or other big challenges—I know I will survive and thrive. I know this because of what the school of entrepreneurship has taught me about my resiliency and my power—which, honestly, I did not know I had inside of me before my success. As you go through the school of entrepreneurship, you will develop muscles you never knew you had.

LEARNING LEADS TO OPPORTUNITY

Right after I graduated from university in my early twenties, I decided to go traveling through India. Most of my friends' parents expected them to find a job and to start working right away since they had just spent fortunes paying for their college diplomas. But my dad said, "Great idea. Traveling is the best education." (Yes, I had an extraordinary father.) He knew that learning extended far beyond the walls of a school. That trip to India might have been one of the reasons I had the interest and confidence to travel to Indonesia in my thirties—seeds were planted that started to blossom ten years later.

Always seek learning, as it will lead you to your next steps. This is why your primary job as the CEO of your business is to be a ferocious learner.

In addition to having a passion and a hunger to learn and grow, what else does it mean to be a ferocious learner? It simply means making learning a priority in your life—*always*. It means that you do not stop learning—*ever*. Through learning, you'll get new ideas, you'll meet inspiring people, and you will be comfortable with all things financial in nature including reading those profit and loss statements I mentioned earlier. Deliberately choosing to continuously learn is one of the master keys because it's an investment that you can count on to lead to your success—not only your success in business but your success in life!

Again, the idea that "it's never too late" applies here. If you live to be 110 years old, and you keep learning and growing for all the days of your life from this point forward, imagine how rich the rest of your life will be.

I received an email from my mom recently that I just love. She wrote:

> *Leslie, it just came to me who you are and why you are successful. You are out there to listen and are open to learning, even if it may seem contradictory to your own ideas. I will say, very few people have achieved this in life— that is your secret. Love, Mom*

Sometimes I say, in a tongue-in-cheek way, that one of the reasons for my success is I just follow directions from my consultant, Lisa Suttora. I listen to what she says. Then I take action. Of course, there's more to it (including the seven keys in this book), but trusting in her guidance has been instrumental to my business and personal growth.

In his book *The Magic of Thinking Big*, Dr. David Schwartz quoted a successful store owner who said, "It isn't so much what you know when you start that matters. It's what you learn and put to use after you open your doors that counts most." That message is crucial. We often think we can't do something because we don't have the experience, the degree, the training, or enough knowledge. But this is one of the biggest traps of all. What matters most is what you *will* learn, then what you *do* with that learning.

Remember, you are the captain of your business ship, and it is up to you to steer it so it doesn't hit any rocks or icebergs. To do that, you need a map. Learning is your map.

As a kick-ass entrepreneur, here are seven powerful ways to learn.

HIRE A KICK-ASS COACH

Investing in a coach is the fastest and smartest route to your success. However, you don't want to hire just any kind of coach. As I did with Lisa, *you want to hire a coach who was where you are now and is where you want to be.* You probably don't want to hire a coach who has just completed coaching school. You want to hire a coach who has already been successful and can show you how to be successful too. We need people in our lives who can mirror success for us.

In my case, Lisa was a highly successful Amazon and eBay seller and a sought-after speaker at e-commerce conferences. She had taken the journey from "beginner" to "expert." I was hungry for knowledge and knew I could trust her to guide me.

I understand that for those who are just starting their business or are not yet profitable, being able to afford a coach may seem daunting. I address this further in Chapter 9, including suggestions for tangible action steps that can put this kind of investment within your reach.

LISTEN TO PODCASTS

Podcasts offer a fabulous way to learn everything you want for free. Many of the great business mentors out there use their podcasts as a way to offer free content and then enroll you into one of their paid services or to buy a course or book. I'll happily admit I am a podcast junky and rarely drive anywhere without listening to one of my favorites. I find them uplifting, and they give me a quick hit of ideas and inspiration. I have several in my podcast menu, and here are the five I listen to regularly:

Glambition Radio with **Ali Brown.** This podcast is my go-to for inspiration and motivation as a women entrepreneur. Ali interviews high-revenue women entrepreneurs who tell it like it is, speaking of both the struggles and the triumphs. Ali's show is also entertaining. It's like snuggling up for an in-depth conversation with your favorite girlfriends, who also happen to be really smart and financially prosperous.

Capitalism.com with **Ryan Daniel Moran.** Buckle your seat belt for a highly original approach to business and making money. An expert in building physical product brands, Ryan is authentic, vulnerable, and wise. His motto is "Build a business, invest the profits," and he teaches you how to do both with an added emphasis on how you can improve the world in the process.

Rock Your Brand with **Scott Voelker.** Scott offers easy-to-follow, step-by-step information on how to build your online brand. His clear and direct motto is "Take action," and he shows you how.

Online Marketing Made Easy with **Amy Porterfield.** Many of the brand-building teachers out there are men, so I find Amy's feminine style of teaching more relatable. She is an excellent mentor for audience-building and launching digital courses.

The Life Coach School with **Brooke Castillo.** Brooke is the coach who does $50 million in revenue I mentioned in Chapter 3. Vulnerable, honest, and smart, Brooke uses her podcast to cover issues around mindset as it applies to all aspects of life such as relationships, money, health, and personal happiness.

TAKE ONLINE COURSES

Sometimes you need more than what a free podcast can give you. Online courses can range from twenty dollars to thousands of dollars. They are often taught live and include downloadable information and homework. Oftentimes, the sessions or modules are recorded, and you can listen (or re-listen) when it is convenient for you.

A few courses I have taken have literally changed my life for the better. One of them was **Feminine Power**, Dr. Claire Zammit's program that I mentioned in Chapter 4. Until taking that course, I had only been working on my business and not sharing anything I had learned. This was causing me to feel invisible, like I only lived behind my computer screen (can you relate?). After taking the course, I started giving speeches on the topic of creating a successful business on Amazon.com and teaching the Amazon-focused workshop I wrote about in Chapter 2, both of which I had been yearning to do.

The Book Doulas' Incubator Program with Kristine Carlson and Debra Evans is a fabulous book-writing course and the reason you are reading this book right now. Their course started me on my path to putting words on the page (via my computer) and finishing all eleven chapters. In the process, I discovered how much I adore writing.

Lifebook presented by Mind Valley, an online education platform, is another course I have taken that has had a strong influence. With Lifebook, you take the time to focus on the goals you have for every aspect of your life. It helped me to not only get clearer on my business goals, but it helped me to widen my view and identify other goals that are important to me.

If online marketing and brand-building are important to you, here are the rock star experts to learn from: Lisa Suttora, Ryan Daniel Moran, Scott Voelker, Amy Porterfield, and Steve Chou. Google away. Dig into the courses, programs, and other services they offer. I personally know each one of them, and I know you will be in great hands.

JOIN FACEBOOK GROUPS

Private Facebook groups are another excellent way to learn. They are private because you have to apply to be part of them. Once you do, your friends and family will not see anything you post within the group space. Only the other private members will be able to see your posts.

You can find the groups that resonate with you by doing a search on Facebook that includes keywords on your topic. For example, when I was looking for a private group for women entrepreneurs, I simply typed the keywords *women + entrepreneurs*. I also did a narrower search when I wanted to find a group for women who sell products online, typing in *women + selling online + successful*. If I wanted to join a private group for healthy eating, I would type in *nutrition + healthy eating* or *healthy lifestyle*. You can try lots of different keyword combinations to see what comes up.

I like the private groups because you can make great connections with people and ask them questions. People love to help, and often, they offer specific and strategic suggestions. It's also a wonderful way to share what you know and help someone else. Many of the stories in this book came from women in one of my own private Facebook groups. In exchange for my counsel, they shared with me their entrepreneurial journeys—a win-win for both of us.

ATTEND IN-PERSON OR VIRTUAL CONFERENCES

The power of going to an in-person conference is hard to beat. The opportunity to meet, talk, brainstorm, possibly share a meal—it's enlivening, fun, and great for sparking new ideas and forging new alliances. I find conferences to be thrilling, like going on a date you really want to go on. As entrepreneurs, we often work from home and have few reasons to put on nice clothes or makeup. Even with online conferences, we only need to make an effort from the waist up. But when you go to an in-person conference, it feels good to wear pretty shoes, spend some time on your hair, and enjoy a change of environment.

The number of creative ideas you will be exposed to and absorb at either type of conference can be staggering. As author Dr. Schwartz says, "Remember, a mind that feeds only on itself soon is undernourished, becoming weak and incapable of creative progressive thought. Stimulation from others is excellent mind food." Mind food is exactly what you get at a conference or workshop.

In addition to the ideas these meetings can generate, you can also make long-lasting connections with others. When you do connect with someone, be sure to keep it alive. For example, every few months I have a Zoom call with a woman I met at a conference a few years ago. We talk about courses we're taking, books we've read or listened to, coaches we've worked with, and the ups and downs of running our businesses. It has been wonderful to build not just a professional relationship but a personal one as well.

READ INSPIRING BUSINESS AND PERSONAL GROWTH BOOKS

As the beloved children's book author Dr. Seuss says, "The more that you read, the more things you will know. The more that you learn, the more places you'll go." Books open up new worlds to us. They spark the imagination and invite us to consider possibilities we may never have thought of before.

One book can literally change your life. Maybe you've had that experience already somewhere along the way, and if so, I want to affirm it can happen again

...and again.

Here is a short list of some of my favorite business and mindset books:

- *Think and Grow Rich* by Napoleon Hill: The mothership of mindset training. Even though it is dated, the wisdom in this book is profound. I believe if every person on earth read and applied this book, it would be a much better place.
- *See You at the Top* by Zig Ziglar: As I described in Chapter 2, this book is a classic on the topic of mindset and success. Zig offers a heartfelt blend of common sense and practical information that will inspire you greatly.

- *Profit First* by Mike Michalowicz: A gold mine, which we first discussed in Chapter 2. Teaches you how to allocate your revenue so you always pay yourself first.
- *Rich Dad Poor Dad* by Robert Kiyosaki: A completely brilliant and alternative way of looking at investing. Following his guidance will give you wealth.
- *Sacred Success: A Course in Financial Miracles* by Barbara Stanny: Gives you a proven process that combines the practical and spiritual without sacrificing your values.
- *Blue Ocean Strategy: How to Create Uncontested Market Space and Make the Competition Irrelevant* by W. Chan Kim: Teaches you to think outside the box and will open your mind to possibilities you may not have considered otherwise.
- *12 Months to $1 Million: How to Pick a Winning Product, Build a Real Business, and Become a Seven-Figure Entrepreneur* by Ryan Daniel Moran, the dynamo whose podcast I recommended previously. This is the best book I know of for step-by-step instruction on how to sell on Amazon and build raving fans.
- *The Take Action Effect: Proven Steps to Build a Future-proof Business & Create Your Ultimate Freedom* by Scott Voelker. Gives you a down-to-earth and practical guide on building brands and audiences.

JOIN A MASTERMIND GROUP

Napoleon Hill said, "No two minds ever come together without thereby creating an invisible, intangible force which may be likened to a third mind." Another way to say this is, two heads are better than one.

Being an entrepreneur can feel lonely at times, perhaps especially for us women who are wired to connect. We thrive on talking with each other—listening, sharing, and supporting. I would go so far as to say that without positive female connections, we suffer. As an entrepreneur, it is especially important to find other women *entrepreneurs* to connect with, to share your business concerns, challenges, and triumphs with someone who really gets it.

I joined a mastermind group several years ago, which we named The Naked Illuminators. We chose the name to affirm our commitment to being transparent and honest with each other. Once a month, four of us come together online to learn from and support each other. Our group is diverse, with each of us being from a different country and having different cultural and ethnic backgrounds. Our topics cover just about everything: thinking big, money, creativity, business partnerships, marketing, healthy lifestyle tips, and even sex. I told you, we get naked! These three women have become more than a support system; they are my most cherished and valued friends.

I highly encourage you to become part of a mastermind group. First, I recommend a group size of not more than four because when you meet—whether in-person or online—you want to be able to conduct your meeting in under ninety minutes. If you have too many women in the group, there simply will not be enough time. One of the great benefits of being part of a highly intentional group is that you are holding yourself accountable for the things you say you will do—the objectives, goals, and milestones you set for yourself and how you will reach them. Also, as my group can attest to, being part of a mastermind will give you a sense of belonging, and we all need and deserve that wonderful feeling.

QUICK REVIEW

You are moving along beautifully now. You've learned about Key #1—the power of really wanting it, Key #2—the importance of focusing on what you want, and now Key #3, where I hope I've ignited your passion for continuously learning and growing. The rewards and benefits will last for the rest of your life.

WHERE WE'RE GOING NEXT

It's time now to learn Key #4, something so powerful, it can literally save your life, as it did mine. Turn the page to find out what that is.

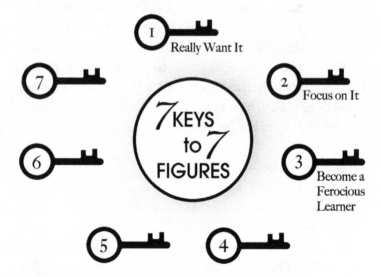

Chapter 7

KEY #4: MASTER YOUR THOUGHTS

"Whether you think you can or can't, you're right."
—HENRY FORD

Your thoughts are so powerful that they can literally influence whether you live or die. I can tell you this is true with complete certainty because I experienced it firsthand.

On a cold, gray, late-November day, when I was in my early thirties, I was visiting friends who had a lake house in Long Island, New York. I had come there with Ben (not his real name), a beautiful man I had recently met and fallen deeply in love with.

We had been indoors for most of the day, Ben playing guitar and me playing piano, as we tried together to play Billy Joel's "Uptown Girl." Around 4:00 p.m., we noticed the canoe on the lawn near the water, and needing some fresh air, we thought it would be fun to take the boat out to paddle around on the lake.

The lake was beautiful and large, and on this day, the water was calm. Pushing off the dock, two swans floated alongside us. I was sitting in the rear of the canoe and Ben was in the front with his back toward me with one ore in his hands. As is often the case in November, the sky was heavy with clouds, the air was chilly, and there on the lake the feeling was very peaceful.

Then everything changed.

Ben made a quick and strong movement with the ore to the left, which made the tip of the canoe swing violently to the left and caused us to sway to the right. The canoe then swung to the right, we swung to the left, and we were both thrust out of the boat into the water.

We were fully dressed in jeans, boots, sweaters, and leather jackets. The water was frigid—there was even a bit of ice along the banks. The early winter sun was setting, and even though there was light, it was quickly getting darker. We decided to swim for the shore. We could see lights at a distance and the shore seemed to be within reach.

Almost immediately and for reasons I don't know, we were separated. Maybe it was the tide; I'm not sure. My leather jacket feeling heavy in the water, I took it off. I tried to swim without knowing which direction I needed to go. My instinct just said, "Go!" Ben yelled to me, "You are going in the wrong direction!"

I could barely move with all that clothing on, and without really realizing it, I began to feel very relaxed and drowsy—a dangerous symptom I learned later was one of the advanced stages of hypothermia. The water felt oddly warm, and as I lay on the water on my back, moving my legs just a bit, the clouds above my head seemed to be getting closer and closer. I felt myself drifting off. It felt beautiful. Peaceful. Silent. Warm. As I floated there in this silence, no longer swimming toward any direction, something inside of me woke up with a start.

Alarm.

Out of nowhere, out of the quiet, the peace, the silence, the calmness, something rose from the deepest place within me.

"There is no fucking way I am dying in this water! No way!" I yelled out loud.

I had recently learned chanting meditation, and I began to chant a mantra, repeating it over and over and over again. I struggled to keep myself awake and above water through an intense focus on thoughts of surviving while chanting the mantra. I didn't know where I was or if I was getting closer to the shore. All I knew was to keep doing what I was doing.

Then, somehow, someway, my hands touched weeds, and I knew I had gotten to shore. In a moment, I found myself sitting in the shallow water.

By this time, it was dark, and I could no longer see Ben. I did see lights on in a nearby house, and I struggled to stand and scrambled my way there, banging on the door for help. Ambulances arrived, and I was whisked off to the hospital.

Ben had been found, but he did not make it. My beautiful friend lost his life that day.

Later, a nurse told me it was a miracle I survived and that normally people cannot live in the kind of low temperatures we were in for more than ten minutes. I was in the water for twenty-five minutes. I don't know what other forces were in play that day, nor do I know why I lived and my friend died, but I can tell you this: I was given a choice that day to live or die, and it was my ferocious declaration—*there is no fucking way I am dying in this water*—that saved my life. I cannot say for sure what else was involved in the making of my miracle. Maybe it just wasn't my time. But I do know that my powerful mind, my thoughts of surviving and refusing to give up, played a significant role.

Mourning Ben's death took a long time. It was a great shock that marked the end of a certain kind of youthful innocence for me. But his warmth, kindness, and enthusiasm for life have remained with me. In honor of him, I share this story with you to drive home how powerful our thoughts are and how much they influence our life. I am living proof of this and grateful that I get to spread this message.

If you have ever thought that all this mindset and positive thinking stuff is airy-fairy, New Age garbage—and I can understand if you do, as the term "mindset" has become so widely used these days that it has lost much of its meaning and power—I hope I've changed your mind. There is nothing more powerful *that you can control* than your own thoughts. Your thoughts are so powerful that they can literally keep you alive.

THOUGHTS ARE THINGS

What does any of this have to do with your business and being successful? Everything. Your thoughts are so powerful that they *will* make or break your business. The thoughts you have about yourself and what you think you can or cannot accomplish will determine the outcome of everything in your life, including how much money you will make and how successful your business will be. Your thoughts will be aligned with whether you believe you can actually have what you really want, desire, and yearn for.

You've heard this idea before: thoughts are things. They are living, dynamic, influential, powerful forces. Thoughts are what kept me alive in that cold water, and thoughts are what created my now-successful business. Your thoughts are influencing your life, your business, and how much money you have right now.

There is nothing that exists in this world that did not start as a thought. Think of the wonder of this! Right now, look around the room you are in, wherever you may be. Notice anything that is there—the table, the rug, the painting, the warm glow of the lamp. Every one of these things started with someone's thought. The job or business you have now began with a thought. Likewise, the business you want to have will start with a thought. As Buddha said, "All that we are is the result of what we have thought. The mind is everything. What we think, we become."

Thoughts create the underlying belief system that is operating inside of you. What's even more amazing is that according to research done by Dr. Claire Zammit, 80 percent of what we call "our experience" comes from inside of us, and only 20 percent comes from external circumstances. The great majority of what we *think* is happening in our lives is being created not from what is occurring in our outer world but by what is happening inside our heads and of what we *think* about what is happening—whether or not it is true. Wow, that is a mind *fluck*!

MASTER YOUR BRAIN, MASTER YOUR THOUGHTS

The National Science Foundation published an article summarizing research on the daily thoughts of human beings. It showed that the average person has about 12,000 to 60,000 thoughts per day. Isn't that mind-blowing! Of those thousands of thoughts, 80 percent were found to be negative, and 95 percent were exactly the same repetitive thoughts as the day before. Just let those numbers land.

Barbara Huson's book *The Rewire Response* builds a case that all thoughts, when repeated often, literally change the physiology of the brain. She says that when the same thought is restated in our mind over and over again, it literally creates a physical impression in our brain. In the same way the ring you wear has created a physical impression on your finger or the way a stream cuts through rock once it has been flowing there for many years, your repetitive thoughts, whether positive or negative, create similar furrows and impressions on your brain. The thoughts we think over and over again—whether they are supportive or destructive to us—become our own personal norm.

Consciously deciding what you want your norm to be is synonymous with mastery of your thoughts. Negative or limiting thoughts are the reason you may not yet be taking the necessary steps to grow your business or start the business you've been dreaming of. They are the reason you haven't quit the job you no longer love. They're the reason your business is idling in mediocrity. They're the reason your bank account looks like the way it does. They're the reason you are still waiting and hoping something will change. Again, I've been there. There have been long periods of time wherein I completely forgot some of the most important lessons I learned upon surviving that day on the lake. But the amnesia wore off eventually, and I came to embrace the powerful gifts I had been given—one of those gifts being the deep-in-my-soul knowing that I am responsible for my thoughts and their immense creative power. I run toward the understanding that being a grown-up powerful woman starts with putting on those big girl panties and taking 100 percent responsibility for where I am right now. I love that I finally got over believing that I didn't have control over my thinking, because I do. And so do you.

I know this is not easy. Even now, as I write this book, something I am doing in my sixties, I have had thoughts like these beauties:

Who am I to write a book?

Why bother to write this book? There are so many other business success books out there written by well-known people.

I already have a successful business that makes money. Why write a book and make myself vulnerable by telling the world what a failure I use to feel like?

If I had followed those fear-based thoughts (and others just like them), I wouldn't have experienced the joy of the writing process and you would not be reading this book right now.

So what did I do to change my thinking? For one thing, I put myself fully in charge. I decided my burning desires mattered *more* than my doubts and deserved to be fulfilled. One of my biggest burning desires is to help you to become a highly successful, money-making, freedom-loving entrepreneur, and there was just no way I was going to let my negative thoughts douse that flame.

It's extremely common to have negative thoughts and to be disparaging about our own abilities. This is sadly one of the afflictions of being human. I don't think my cat ever thinks about whether or not he's living up to his cat potential—he just is who he is and knows he is great! But we humans suffer terribly from negative thinking. And we women suffer from this a lot more than the guys do, and it starts early in life.

THE FEMALE CONFIDENCE FACTOR

As I discussed earlier, I used to run Girl Power, my empowerment program for girls from seven to thirteen years old, giving me a front-row seat to witnessing how girls think about themselves.

When we were focusing on the topic of positive thinking, we would sit in a circle on pillows with a big bowl of popcorn in the middle to share. It was a cozy and supportive place. I would ask the girls to write down five thoughts about themselves that were "not so nice." They never had trouble doing this and would scribble away, easily coming up with many derogatory thoughts. However, when I would ask them to write down positive thoughts they had about themselves, they'd struggle to come up with five. After working with hundreds of girls over the years, I saw that there were three negative thoughts that came up repeatedly:

No one likes me.

I am stupid.

I am ugly.

Sad, isn't it? These are eight-, ten-, twelve-year-old girls thinking this way about their beautiful, irreplaceable selves. I did some digging into the research on the self-esteem and confidence of girls and found these concerning statistics: 45 percent of girls and 55 percent of boys in grammar school indicate that they have high self-esteem by saying they are "good at a lot of things." But in middle school, only 20 percent of girls say this compared to 46 percent of boys. Self-esteem in girls going through puberty drops by more than 50 percent, and only 15 percent in boys.

According to an article in *Forbes*, gender differences in confidence for adult women are quite dramatic. A study done at Cornell University found that while women underestimate their abilities and performance, men overestimate them, even though there is no difference in the quality and quantity of the performance. Interesting, isn't it? Clinical psychologists Dr. Pauline Clance and Dr. Suzanne Imes coined the term "impostor syndrome," which goes hand in hand with these research findings. Women frequently express that they don't feel they deserve their job and fear being "found out" at any moment—expecting to be unmasked as an impostor or fraud. Drs. Clance and Imes found that women worry more about being disliked, appearing unattractive, outshining others, or grabbing too much attention.

Can you relate? Sadly, I can.

This one really sums it up. A Hewlett-Packard internal report found that men apply for a job or promotion when they meet only 60 percent of the qualifications, but women apply only if they meet 100 percent of them. What sometimes dooms women is not our actual abilities but rather the decision not to try.

I can *so* relate to that. How about you?

Sometimes we truly believe we are all alone with these thoughts in our heads—*I'm not liked, I'm not talented enough, I hate my thighs.* (By the way, these thoughts are eerily similar to the ones the young girls had.) Even with all of our life experience and wisdom, we imagine that certain women—those who appear to have it all together—don't have negative thoughts about themselves. But they do.

We're complex creatures. We can be confident and courageous and still have moments of doubt or vulnerability. Imagine one of the many public conversations between Oprah and Gayle King, two extraordinarily powerful and accomplished women. Maybe you've watched some of them on television or online. Their willingness to share their mountaintop moments of success and their deep valley moments of doubt and fear is an empowering reminder that we're all multifaceted. Self-esteem, self-respect, and self-confidence aren't static aspects of who we are and what we think and feel.

There are many women who have high self-esteem and confidence, but maybe they weren't born with those qualities fully intact. Perhaps that describes most of us. These traits grow and strengthen over time. Sometimes our confidence grows because of what we've gone through and sometimes despite it. We're each wired differently. But for the great majority of us, I would say that confidence is hard-won.

One thing I know for sure is that it's powerfully influenced by the stories inside our own heads that we tell ourselves again and again.

THE STORIES IN OUR HEADS

These stories, whether we are conscious of them or not, are influencing our lives, our decisions, our choices, and our actions. Here are some common narratives:

- Life is hard.
- Without a degree, I can expect to get only so far.
- You're either born with talent or you're not.
- It's impossible to earn that much money.
- I didn't have any successful role models growing up.
- I wasn't born into wealth.
- Some people are just lucky.
- I don't have connections.
- I have to accept my fate.
- It's too late to change it.
- It's too late to change me.

And on and on and on. Can you relate to any of these storylines?

When I was working to master my own thoughts, before I became successful, I did an exercise where I wrote down a bunch of thoughts I truly believed and thought were 100 percent correct yet I could see were limiting my life. Here is a sampling of them in all their "glory":

I can either be spiritual, or I can have nice things.

I can either have a gorgeous, expensive apartment, or I can have an easy life with low expenses.

I can either work hard, or I can be more peaceful and free.

I can either be very successful, or I can be more feminine.

Wow! Now there is some classic either-or thinking! I decided to rewrite them and play with the new idea of having both at the same time. This is what I came up with:

I can live in a drop-dead gorgeous apartment, decorated beautifully, and have an easy life with very low expenses.

I can have a successful business and have lots of time for being, writing, walking, and having fun.

I can feel peaceful inside and be successful in the world.

I can be spiritual and have great clothes and look fabulous.

When I dug out the journals where I had written these statements, I had to smile because there it was in blue and white (I'm partial to pens with blue ink)—once again, proof that this "mastering your thoughts" stuff actually works. It was in the writing of this book that I realized that *every single statement* from the positive list has come to pass.

Napoleon Hill, author of the life-changing book *Think and Grow Rich*, said it best: "Whatever the mind of [woman] can conceive and believe, it can achieve." And you, beautiful woman, to achieve what you want, you must master your thoughts so they serve you well.

So how do you harness that untamed horse known as the mind that has a tendency to run wild? How in the world do you *master* your thoughts? Here are four powerful ways.

#1: KNOW WHAT YOUR NEGATIVE THOUGHTS ARE

The first way to master your thoughts is to identify those that are limiting you, holding you back, or causing you to suffer in any way. You have to pull them out from under the rug, metaphorically speaking, because try as we may to keep negative thoughts, beliefs, and ideas buried or hidden, they still influence us. It's like having a scary monster locked up in our basement. Even though it's locked up, it is still posing a threat that makes it hard to sleep peacefully at night. That negative thought monster may be affecting your life and your success more than you realize. The good news is that when you take it out of your mental basement and shine the light of awareness onto it, its ability to control you fades away. (Sidenote: I'm not a big proponent of spending a lot of time rooting around for every negative thought we have about ourselves. That can be counterproductive. We just need to make some of our negative thoughts conscious and trust that the light of our own awareness will neutralize the rest.)

Let's start excavating some of those thoughts from your mental basement utilizing a little trick I learned from one of my mentors, which I've slightly adapted here.

First, make a brief list of negative thoughts you have about yourself, starting with the words "I am."

"I am_____ (fill in the blank with a negative thought)."

"I am_____ (fill in the blank with a negative thought)."

"I am_____ (fill in the blank with a negative thought)."

"I am_____ (fill in the blank with a negative thought)."

Now it's time to make a small but potent adjustment to the thoughts you wrote down. Instead of "I am," start with "The voice of fear says."

"The voice of fear says_____ (fill in the blank with a negative thought)."

"The voice of fear says_____ (fill in the blank with a negative thought)."

"The voice of fear says_____ (fill in the blank with a negative thought)."

"The voice of fear says_____ (fill in the blank with a negative thought)."

For example, "I am not good enough" becomes "The voice of fear says I am not good enough." In this way, you've put some space between you and the thought. You've created a boundary with the negativity that provides a new perspective. The negative belief can be seen for what it is—just a thought—not who you are. Because, beautiful woman, you are good enough, and the voice of fear holds no real power over you.

#2: BE VIGILANT WITH THE WORDS THAT COME OUT OF YOUR MOUTH

Whoever said "Sticks and stones can break your bones, but words can never hurt you" is wrong. Words can hurt a lot. Words can even devastate. I once heard a wise teacher say that with our words, we can destroy in less than one minute what we've spent years building and growing, like a relationship. So yes, just like the thoughts we think are powerful, so are the words that pass through our lips. When it comes to the relationship we have with ourselves and the way we live our lives, our words have a great deal to do with whether we succeed or fail, whether we are happy or unfulfilled.

I'm constantly correcting my language because I know the power of words. I'm committed to not making negative comments about my business, and when I do, I quickly correct myself. This has been a regular practice now for several years. When I was still making only $50,000 a year in online revenue, I frequently corrected my language about my business, changing it to something positive. Instead of saying, "I'm worried my business won't work; there's too much competition online" (which could be true or not), I would say, "My business is so successful; it is just mind-blowing."

As I began writing this book, we were all in the early stages of the worldwide COVID-19 pandemic, and the state of the economy was alarming. There were all kinds of fears that I could have voiced. I could have said, "The economy is awful; my business will go *down*," but I knew that I didn't have to go down that road. Here's what I said instead:

"Yes, the economy is awful, but my business will go up."

"I am going to have the most profitable year ever!"

"The truth is, at this very moment, in the middle of this challenging economy, there are businesses doing their highest revenues ever. Who's to say that mine won't too? I'm saying it will."

Some people might say, "Well, that is not very realistic." But until something happens one way or the other, it is just as unrealistic to align with the negative outcomes. Therefore, why not give yourself the most positive and uplifting statements—the ones that energize you and propel you forward with optimism?

Right about the time I got serious about growing my business, I heard a great affirmation that I decided to say to myself every day: *Money comes easily and frequently.* As significant growth started to happen, I added the words "a lot of" to the sentence: *A lot of money comes easily and frequently.* Not only did this become a daily mantra for me, but my husband repeats this sentence daily as well. If you feel the call, I invite you to use this mantra for yourself and find out how good it can make you feel. Say it out loud each day:

"A lot of money comes easily and frequently."

With each word you utter, you are putting out a directive. You might as well choose words that serve you instead of those that perpetuate failure. Stand guard over your dreams and watch the words that come out of your mouth about yourself, your business, and your life. Be a vigilante defending the greatest treasure in the world—*you*. Seriously! We have only one of you.

#3: IMMERSE YOURSELF IN INSPIRATION

We need as much help as we can to keep our thoughts and words positive, and the best way to do so is to surround yourself with positive and inspiring influences in the form of books, podcasts, and people. I recommend devoting a portion of each day to absolutely inundating yourself with inspiration.

I love this kind of purposeful immersion. It's no chore for me to read or listen to something that will lift me up. Every day, I read a passage from one of the mindset books I mentioned in the previous chapter on being a ferocious learner (Key #3), such as *Think and Grow Rich*, a perennial favorite of mine.

It's helpful to figure out what time of day you are most receptive to inspiration. Is it in the morning, in the evening, in the middle of the day? My favorite time to listen to podcasts is while driving. Maybe for you, it's when you're walking around your neighborhood with your earphones in, or when you're curled up in your favorite chair.

As you know, people can lift you up or put you down, which is why choosing who is near you is so important. I know this can be hard. We can find ourselves around family members or coworkers who tend to be negative. But when we bring more awareness to noticing who we're spending most of our time with, positive change happens. We gradually become more discerning and decisive. When I was in my twenties and thirties, I had several "friends" who simply didn't lift me up. Now that I am older, I only have people in my circle who love me and who feel good to be around. This, of course, goes both ways. I'm now a more uplifting presence in the lives of my family, friends, colleagues, and clients than I was back then.

The bottom line: When you immerse yourself in inspiration, you are an ever-expanding source of inspiration!

#4 PRACTICE FEELING GOOD EACH DAY

Imagine your life if you made feeling good one of your top goals every day of the week. When you feel good, it's easier to be positive. Feeling good literally raises your happy hormones and has an effect on your whole body. Think about the things that make you feel good and that you can easily do. Make a list if you'd like. (Spoiler: These activities or experiences are usually simple and free.)

For me, feeling good includes starting my day with a pot of jasmine green tea and sipping it out of my grandmother's beautiful green-and-cream-colored china cups. It's sitting with my husband over a coffee and talking about our future. It's being in nature and sitting near moss while looking at a stream. It's petting my cat. For me, feeling good often involves dancing. These are my favorite feel-good activities. What are yours?

Another way to feel good is to set yourself up to always win. My friend Sally is a master at this. For example, she wanted to learn German and decided that success to her was learning just one word a month! In achieving her monthly goal, she made herself feel like a linguistic genius. Sally kept her commitment and felt good about herself. And over time, she became proficient in German.

You get the idea. Through your goals, plans, and resources, set yourself up to succeed and then celebrate your wins. *Hurray, I cooked dinner!* Or, *Hurray, I finished that project. I'm brilliant! How did I get so fabulous?* See what I mean? You are the one setting up what winning means. Make it as easy as possible, and say lots of nice things to yourself about yourself. As author and transformational teacher Shakti Gawain said, "If you believe yourself to be beautiful, you become so." I like that one!

A MILLIONAIRE MINDSET

Your business begins with your mind. In the beginning, it was my thoughts about not getting a job coupled with remembering the gorgeous clothing I saw in Bali that began the creation process of the business I now have. Your thoughts have brought you to the business you have or the one you want to create, and they will allow your business to evolve and flourish over time as you continue to harness them.

Also, the power of your thoughts is ageless. Whether you are twenty or seventy, the thoughts in your head and the words that come out of your mouth are a choice—your choice. Choosing thoughts in alignment with your heart's true desires is a creative act of immense power. Wayne Dyer knew this when he said, "Change the way you look at things, and the things you look at will change."

QUICK REVIEW

Let's recap where we are. Key #1 is Really Want It, where you get clear on your burning desire and yearnings. Key #2 is all about implementing the power of focus and understanding that multitasking will not bring you the success you want. Key #3 encourages you to become a ferocious learner and includes a smorgasbord of ideas to feed your hunger to grow and expand. And now you have Key #4, which is the invitation to master your thoughts, because your thinking *will* determine the success of your business.

WHERE WE'RE GOING NEXT

It's time now to get some work done. Turn the page to gain access to Key #5 and find out how it will make your business soar.

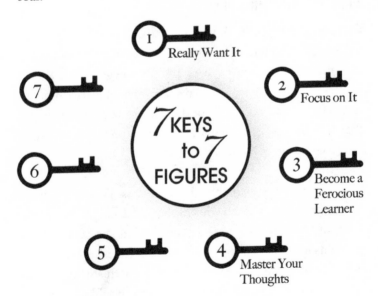

Chapter 8

KEY #5: TAKE ACTION AND SOAR

"Nothing will work unless you do."
—MAYA ANGELOU

To enjoy having a seven-figure business (or even a six-figure business), a lot of action is required. All the wanting, focusing, learning, and positive thinking will go to waste if you don't take action and actually *do* something. Long before Nike caught on to it, one of my dad's favorite sayings was "Just do it," and when it comes to getting results, those three words are like rocket fuel, helping to bring your vision to fruition.

But "doing" is where many of us get stuck. There are so many things that need to be done—developing products or services (or both), creating a sales and marketing strategy, managing social media, handling the many details related to operations and finances, just to name the basics. Where do you start? What is most important? And do you have the tools and resources in place to take the necessary steps?

Annette Karlen, a dynamic young woman who recently started a marketing company for the financial industry, enlisted my support as she prepared to launch. She told me in our first consulting session that she was totally overwhelmed by trying to figure out what she needed to do first. Everything seemed equally important. This crisis of prioritization is typical of what most entrepreneurs experience. Believe me, I've been there and know how disempowering it can be. For me, it felt bad enough that it became a big catalyst for absolutely mastering this aspect of business. I learned there are certain operational activities that, when done, are the cornerstone to getting out of overwhelm and running a thriving business. This chapter is an outgrowth of those discoveries and it's going to be an invaluable tool for you—a mini guidebook to help you to take action and soar.

Ready?

Great, let's go!

THE ENTREPRENEURIAL POWER COUPLE: INNER ACTIONS AND OUTER ACTIONS

There are two categories of actions that need to be taken in order to realize success in our businesses. There are *inner actions* and *outer actions*. Both are essential as interdependent forces. Like the yin-yang symbol of ancient Taoist teachings, they complete each other. When inner and outer actions are equally valued and prioritized, they come together to produce results of greater impact.

Think of it this way. The *inner actions* you take come together as the powerful feminine force that creates your business. The inner actions create your intentions, they birth your longings and burning desire for your business, and they are the force that will make your entrepreneurial dreams manifest. The *outer actions* you take come together as the powerful masculine force that accomplishes tasks. In other words, outer actions comprise your to-do list.

Most businesses attempt to run *only* on outer actions, and they ignore or simply have no knowledge of the importance of the inner actions. That, beautiful woman, is where *we* are different. We use the power of our inner actions to germinate the business we want to create and call forth our intentions.

When we focus on only outer actions, we get tangled up in the nonstop doing and pushing and exhaustion that we want to avoid.

INNER ACTIONS: THE MIRACLE MAKERS

The foundation of all businesses is generating money by making sales of a product or service. Businesses without sales are called hobbies, and we are not in the hobby business. We are in the "make money and live your freedom" business. In order to make sales, we need to start with an intention of what we would *love* our sales to be.

Sidenote: If you doubt the power of this inside-out approach, consider Oprah's words—"The principle of intention is literally what saved and changed the trajectory of my life." What more proof do we need than that? Clarifying our intentions for the money we want to make and having an inspiring vision for the business we want to devote our time, energy, and love to are essential keys to success.

Why are intentions and vision essential? Because clarifying and reflecting on them connects us with our higher self, our spiritual guides, and our own innately intuitive nature. The fact that we're calling on unseen forces doesn't make them less real. To the contrary, this co-creative power is perhaps the most real power we have. Just think of it as your upstairs team! Your upstairs team is always there to help you to bring forth what you want. But just like with any team-building process, you have to communicate. Your upstairs team is only going to assist in the work when you tell them what you want them to do. Your permission is paramount. Once you ask for support and give the green light, you're paving the way for miracles to occur.

Here are three miracle-making activities you can incorporate by making them a part of the foundation of your inner-action work.

1. THE INTENTION-SETTING MIRACLE

Sit quietly with your journal or paper and pen nearby. Close your eyes and allow yourself to access the state of feeling connected to your inner guidance and intuition. Allow yourself to be open to discovering how this connectedness feels to you uniquely. It could be a feeling of enthusiasm, optimism, anticipation, peace, calm, or another uplifting experience.

Once you feel connected, think about the big vision you have for your business. There's no pressure to get into the details of your vision yet—you'll be doing that in activity #3. For now, go for the "broad strokes," with an emphasis on how you want to *feel* and more specifically, how you want your success in business to feel. Try on a few sentences that exemplify your vision and the feelings that go with it. How would you like to define and describe them? What statement will you declare to the universe and to yourself? For example, it could be something like this:

My business is a total success that grows and grows. There is no end to the possibilities for making a difference and allowing more and more wealth. I feel so much joy and gratitude for the money and freedom I create for my family and myself.

Grab your journal or paper and pen and write down your statement. Memorize each sentence. Each day, read your statement and think of it. Repeat it as often as you like. This statement is your master intention. Let yourself feel the power of it and know it is true.

2. THE MIRROR MIRACLE

Stand in front of a mirror and look at yourself. Take a few soft, deep breaths, and look into your amazing eyes. Now speak your intentional statement out loud. Tell yourself in your own words how successful you are and how proud of yourself you are.

Be prepared because this simple activity can be intense. I have cried a few times doing this practice. Surprising feelings and thoughts can arise. If you laugh, it's okay. If you cry, it's okay. If you think it's silly, it's okay. If you think it's a bunch of BS, it's okay. Do it anyway because the results are more than worthwhile. By doing this, the intention you wrote on paper will come to you faster as you amplify the power of your words by stating them verbally.

You are simultaneously reprogramming your thoughts. You are

getting familiar with this idea. The more you say your intention while looking into your own eyes in the mirror, the more comfortable you are going to be really believing it. You are literally changing the physical structure of your brain—rewiring yourself for success. That is why you are saying this to yourself out loud. Your synapses will be alit with the beautiful fireworks that are set off by high-quality, high-vibe thoughts about yourself and your business.

Be sure to really build yourself up. In addition to your intentional statement, tell yourself you are beautiful, brilliant, successful, and strong. For example, something I have said to myself is this:

> *Leslie, you are a total success! You create so much money and provide so many opportunities for others. I am so proud of who you are. You are powerful and inspirational. Thank you for your passion and commitment. I love you so much.*

Don't be shy! This is no place for modesty. Who else is going to do this for you? It's okay to give yourself permission to brag. If you need a nudge, you have my 100 percent permission to really go for it. Brag away!

3. THE POST-IT MIRACLE

This practice, while being an extremely powerful visualization technique, is also an opportunity to get more specific and practical. You are now going to focus on the exact sales numbers you want to create for your business. You are going to figure out what you *intend* for your sales to be.

First, you'll decide what you want your yearly sales figure to be. Be sure to come up with a figure that is exciting but also believable to you. If you are doing $50,000 a year in sales, for example, and you intend to do $10 million, it might be exciting but not really believable—yet. It may simply be too big a leap from where you are right now to where you would like to be soon. Perhaps $100,000 or $200,000 is more believable at this moment. I encourage you to "try on" different numbers and be attentive to how each one feels. Ultimately, the number you land on must have a "wow" feeling to it. It needs to be exhilarating to you, while also being one that you honestly believe to be attainable in the short term.

Once you have that yearly number, break it down into either daily, weekly, monthly, or quarterly sales. Choosing which allotment it will be depends on the type of business you have. For example, Back from Bali is a product-based business with sales happening every day, so the number I write down is the number I intend my daily sales number to be. If you have a service-based business, like a coaching or consultancy business, then perhaps you'll focus on your monthly or quarterly sales goals.

Determining the apportioned number is easy math. For example, if your yearly sales goal is $100,000, then your number is $8,333 a month, or $1,923 a week, or $274 a day. When you break it down, it also becomes more believable and achievable. For many of us, doing $274 a day in sales feels a lot more tangible and practical than the yearly figure of $100,000—the cumulative figure that is twelve months away. Breaking it down into a daily, weekly, monthly, or quarterly sales and income intention is best.

Coming up with your sales numbers will also help you understand exactly how many products or services you need to sell in order to reach them. For example, if you want your yearly revenue to be $100,000 and you have one product that sells for $50, then you know you need to sell the following number of units:

→ 2,000 units a year
→ 500 units a quarter
→ 167 units a month
→ 39 units a week
→ 6 units a day

If you want to do more than $100,000, you know you need to be selling more than six units a day. When you get practical in this way, it helps you to know if you are charging enough, or whether it's time to create another product or provide another service. For example, you may want to create two products instead of offering one. You may have one product that sells for $50 per unit, and your new product may sell for $100 per unit. When you start playing around with your numbers, you begin to see possibilities. You are also looking at the truth of the matter and can take the actions you need to reach your desired goals. This will usually lead to raising prices or figuring out how to sell more units, or both.

Now it's time to have a bit of fun with Post-it notes. I recommend getting a packet of multicolored Post-its and not just settling for the light yellow ones. Once you have your stack, take out a pen or marker and write down your two main numbers on several Post-its: your yearly number and your apportioned

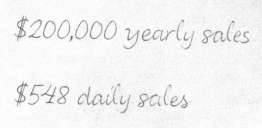

$200,000 yearly sales

$548 daily sales

number (daily, weekly, monthly, or quarterly). Here's an example Post-it:

Write those same numbers on several Post-its. I like to place a Post-it on my bathroom mirror, inside my laptop, in front of my kitchen sink, in the hallway, in my wallet, and on the dashboard of my car. The point is to place this number in front of you all day long. You see it in the morning, you see it walking around your house, you see it while washing dishes, you see it when you're driving, and you see it when you're preparing dinner. Do not underestimate the power of this practice. It will lead to miraculous results.

This is how I built my business. In the early days, I would literally pull up my barstool in my kitchen and just stare at the Post-it in front of my sink. I would just look and look and look, allowing myself to get familiar with the number. The more familiar we are with something, the more believable it becomes. That is what advertisers do. How many times does your Facebook algorithm show you the same ad over and over? It is "brainwashing" you to get comfortable buying that dress, pair of shoes, or training program. This is what you are doing too, but instead of brainwashing yourself to buy another something you may not need, you are brainwashing yourself to pursue your dreams. They say it takes at least seven touch points—the number of times someone comes in contact with the same marketing technique like emails, ads, social media posts, and so forth—for a marketer to hook the customer. For the seven-figure entrepreneur in the making, it takes seven Post-its to reach our intentions!

If you live with people who are supportive of your inner work, by all means keep those Post-its visible. However, if you live with anyone who would make fun of you for using Post-its, don't post them anywhere they can see. In that case, let it be your powerful little secret. Put your Post-its in places others cannot see easily, such as inside your medicine cabinet, inside your wallet, or on the inside of your laptop. In fact, keep all three miracle practices to yourself for now.

If the voice of doubt is whispering to you, telling you that these are lightweight manifesting techniques, I assure you they are not. My multimillion-dollar business is proof they're small but mighty techniques. The entrepreneurs I mentor can tell you the same. As you engage with them fully, you are mastering your thoughts and calling your future toward you.

I recommend practicing the three miracle techniques on a daily basis. You can make it as simple as spending five minutes to connect with your vision and stating your intention out loud (and revising this when it feels like it's time), two minutes looking into your eyes and speaking to yourself in the mirror, then reading your Post-its throughout your day. Easy!

To this day, if you come to my house, you will see little colorful Post-its strategically placed throughout. It gives new meaning to the fashion industry term "color blocking."

OUTER ACTIONS: THE MIRACLE EXPANDERS

Now that you have learned the inner action steps, let's focus on some of the most important outer action steps needed to create a successful business. An old Arabic saying I love states, "Trust in God and tie your camel up." It means, yes, make an intention and trust that the benevolent universe will bring your desired intention to you, but for goodness' sake, at the same time, take personal responsibility through your actions. Tie up your camel so it doesn't wander off, never to be seen again!

When figuring out what those exact outer action steps and tasks are, nothing works better than the tried-and-true to-do list. According to Paula Rizzo, author of *Listful Thinking: Using Lists to Be More Productive, Highly Successful and Less Stressed*, and *Listful Living: A List-Making Journey to a Less Stressed You*, studies show if you write down a task or action step, you're 33 percent more likely to do it. I can attest to the effectiveness of list-making in my own business- and wealth-building, and this is where we're going next.

YOUR "MORE MONEY NOW" TO-DO LIST

First (and obviously), you will need something to write on. I like to use inexpensive 9.5-by-6-inch lined notebooks you can buy in a drugstore or office supply store. If you like to go with something fancier, please do. I used to, but I found it didn't improve my rate of finishing my tasks, so now I just use the cheap ones. The point is to have something to physically write on. I do not recommend making to-do lists on your computer. There is power in actually writing down what you intend to be doing. The field of neuroscience indicates that writing by hand activates large regions of the brain, such as those involved in language, thinking, memorizing, and even healing. In other words, putting pen to paper helps keep us sharp. Plus, as you will see, writing (and later rewriting) your lists cements your intentions.

Start your to-do list by separating out your personal tasks and business tasks. For example, on the left side of my notebook, I write my personal tasks, such as "Buy my nephew a gift" or "Transfer money to my savings." The right side of my notebook has my business tasks. Be sure to keep them separate. "Order more smoothie powder" does not belong with "Research new designs on Amazon" or "Create a lead magnet."

Here is an example of the business side of my to-do list:

- Do an Amazon Live
- Train my new VA

- Follow up on status of new designs
- Research possible influencers to help market
- Send samples to Bali
- Restock bestsellers
- Respond to business emails from my vendors
- Create an email to my customers

I already know I won't be able to finish all of these in one day, so which ones do I do? The best way to decide is to ask myself this question: *Which of these tasks will bring more money now?* Those are the tasks I do first. For me, the answer looks like this:

- Restock bestsellers (going out of stock will hurt my sales)
- Do an Amazon Live (this will make my brand more visible on Amazon, which could lead to more sales)
- Create an email to send to my customers (this will strengthen my relationship with my buyers)

Sure, it would be beneficial to start working with influencers, but it doesn't make it to my top position.

The next step is to figure out how long those three tasks will take. And let me tell you the truth: *they will take so much longer than you ever think they will.* I'll break this down by describing what doing an Amazon Live includes in my world:

- Getting out my lights
- Finding extension cords
- Setting the lights up
- Putting my phone on a stand
- Figuring out the best placement of these things, depending on the weather and the light in my living room

- Choosing the Back from Bali clothing items I'm going to display
- Figuring out what to wear
- Putting on makeup
- Making my hair look presentable
- Making sure my cat is fed so he's not meowing during my live

I know you understand exactly what I'm describing here. And I haven't even done the Amazon Live yet! So yes, most things take much longer than any of us think they will. Keep this high in mind when you get to the next essential step.

SCHEDULE IT

Now it's time to go from handwritten notebook lists to calendaring. Open your favorite online calendar, like Google Calendar or your Mac Calendar, and literally schedule in the tasks, using your most realistic sense of how much time each will require.

Here's an example of mine: I think doing the Amazon Live will take me ninety minutes. Restocking will take me another ninety minutes, and creating an email using Klaviyo, my email service, will take about another seventy-five minutes. On a regular basis, I also schedule time for business emails as I need to respond to my team in Bali, and that is usually another hour. So that is five hours and fifteen minutes to be locked into my calendar.

It's also important to schedule time for taking care of ourselves as well. We need time to eat, make a cup of tea, take a few deep breaths, empty the dishwasher, respond to personal texts and phone calls, and all the other daily personal tasks of life. When can you allot time for these so that you feel good about your self-care?

At the end of the day, cross off each of the tasks on your to-do list that you completed. Then turn to a new page in your notebook and rewrite the tasks you didn't do the day before—again, with your personal to-dos on the left side and the business to-dos on the right side. Then add any new tasks that have come up.

And on it goes.

I normally do this at the start of my day, but you might choose to do this at the end of your day. Even if you're already an ace list-maker, you may want to try it both ways to see which is most effective for you at this stage. Prioritizing these to-dos in your scheduling is a ninja trick, of sorts, because it will help you to get much more done overall. It's energizing and uplifting to know that you're tending to your wealth-building activities.

Once in a while, I fall off the wagon and stop scheduling tasks in my calendar because it does take some effort. Not surprisingly, the feeling of overwhelm creeps up. But when I get back on the scheduling wagon, I feel much more in control. The benefits far outweigh the extra time and attention it takes to schedule your time. Plus, having a record of what you do each day gives you a way to acknowledge and celebrate your accomplishments, whether it's one great accomplishment or ten. Remember, feeling good is what you want to be feeling as you are working, creating, and contributing.

THE BIG-PICTURE WHITEBOARD

I love having a large whiteboard in my home office—also called a dry-erase board—that I can write on and erase with ease. It's so satisfying to see my quarterly sales goals written boldly in this way. For each quarter, I come up with big goals I intend to accomplish over each ninety-day period. I then write them on the whiteboard with a thick marker so that I can see them easily every day.

Q1: January–March: _____

Q2: April–June: _____

Q3: July–September: _____

Q4: October–December: _____

Invest in a whiteboard (usually in the $40–$300 range) and discover the positive impact it will have when used consistently. Just like with the Post-it notes, you are once again imprinting yourself with the visual representation of your intentions. In addition to writing down quarterly sales goals, you can use it to write down other big goals you intend to achieve within ninety days.

Here are five items currently on my whiteboard:

- Get more subscribers on my email list
- Choose and order new samples
- Photograph new samples
- Create more video ads
- Increase my net profit

I purposely write down the general goal, saving the details for my handwritten to-do lists. Will I achieve each goal in ninety days? I intend to, but if I don't, it's okay. I'll add it to the next quarter. We do the best we can, right?

Another way to use the whiteboard, if you prefer a more creative approach, is mind mapping—a wonderful technique you may be familiar with. Mind mapping is a way of creating a visual representation of what you want to achieve in a nonlinear fashion. It is often done using interconnecting (and sometimes overlapping) circles. For example, in my consulting business for mentoring women entrepreneurs, I am using another whiteboard that has a large circle in the center for displaying my big vision and intention: "Helping women rise." Cascading out from that center circle are smaller circles, each one being exciting areas of focus for me: individual mentoring, online courses, writing and selling books, podcasting, and list-building. I love looking at this board as it gives me a clear picture of what

I am creating, and I can add to it anytime a new inspiration comes to me.

POMODORO TECHNIQUE HISTORY

Developer and entrepreneur Francesco Cirillo created the pomodoro technique in the late 1980s when he began to use his tomato-shaped kitchen timer to organize his work schedule. Each working interval is called a pomodoro, the Italian word for tomato.

THE FIVE-STEP POMODORO TECHNIQUE

The following five-step process is a simple yet highly effective way to tend to any one of your daily tasks. It's a way to "chunk" your time, which makes any action step more doable.

One way to experience the effectiveness of this technique is to use it for tasks you've been procrastinating on. Try it and see.

1. Choose your task and total time you'll devote to working on it.

2. Set a timer for twenty-five minutes (either with your phone app or an egg timer).

3. Ready? Go! Work on the task for a solid twenty-five minutes.

4. Take a five-minute break for energy renewal.

5. Start another pomodoro. It can either be the continuation of the task you were just working on, or it can be a brand-new task.

Once you've completed four pomodoros (which is two hours of your time), be sure to take a full twenty- to thirty-minute break before moving on to any other piece of work.

TEAM TIME

I still remember the moment my consultant told me I needed to hire an assistant. I have to say that out of all the fears I have had to overcome as an entrepreneur, hiring someone else topped the list. Hiring someone felt like allowing a stranger to go through my underwear drawer. It felt way too intimate at the time. The truth is, I was afraid they would see I didn't know what I was doing and was indeed an impostor. If I brought them into my business, they would see all my insecurities and weaknesses. Plus, it would take me so much time to teach them what they needed to learn. It just all seemed like one big headache—or nightmare.

But I did it. I decided to stop giving my power away to the voice of fear and hired an assistant. Once I hired her, I couldn't believe how great it was. When we hire someone, we're buying back our time to use in bigger and better ways.

YOUR OPERATIONS LIST

In order to figure out which tasks can be delegated, you first need to know all of the tasks required to run your business. Open an Excel or Google spreadsheet. In the left column, write down every single task needed, no matter how small it may seem. My spreadsheet has a list of 210 tasks. Here's a short sampling of what's included:

- Shipment creation
- Create purchase orders
- Add new videos to YouTube
- Distribute barcodes to vendors
- Validate keyword research

- Social media marketing (Instagram and Facebook)
- Create new ad campaigns
- (And 203 other tasks!)

In the next column, write down your name next to every task that *only* you can do. For example, accessing my bank account to pay my vendors is a task only I can and should do. The empty spaces where there is no name are the tasks for which you are able to hire out and delegate. The tasks that can be delegated are most likely those that are repeated in your business over and over, usually daily. For example, responding to customer emails is a task that needs to be done every day.

For these repetitive and crucial tasks, it's also important to create a document outlining how to do them. This is important because if an assistant who has learned the task is absent for a period of time or is no longer employed by you, there is a written document of your standard operating procedures, or SOPs, for training a new assistant. With your step-by-step SOP, you can systematize tasks, making it easier for everyone involved—those doing the tasks and those on the receiving end of those activities.

Other management tools to consider using when working with assistants are Trello or Asana. Both of these are free online software systems that keep track of the tasks you need your assistant or team to do, allowing you to easily see what has been done and what is not yet done. These systems are wonderful because they eliminate the need to use email to instruct your assistant or team. What a time-saver! Instead, everything is managed in one place.

FINANCE

You know by now that I love money. I am hoping by now that you are allowing yourself to say you do too. Will you take a moment right now and declare out loud that you love money and you want money?

I love money! And I want money!

Good! I hope it makes you smile.

Remember, you are in the money business. One of the main purposes of your business is to make money, so I invite you to make finance your absolute favorite topic! The more money you make, the more fun it is to make money.

Here are the top three components when it comes to your business finances—each one critical for the health and wealth of your enterprise:

- Paying yourself
- Hiring an excellent bookkeeper
- Using online bookkeeping software

When I first started working with my business consultant, Lisa, I'll never forget the conversation when she asked this question: "Do you pay yourself?"

"Well, I use the business money for personal things like trips, clothing, or food," I said.

"No, that is not what I'm asking," she replied. "Do you pay yourself a salary?"

That conversation was revolutionary for me. At that time, I didn't pay myself a salary; I just used the money when there was some extra. *Is that bad?* I wondered. *Isn't that what I'm supposed to do?*

Apparently not.

If you just got a sinking feeling in your gut, know you are not alone. I'm sure there is some startling statistic out there showing most women business owners don't pay themselves a salary, and if they do pay themselves something, it is the leftovers, after they have paid everyone else. Sound familiar?

In Chapter 2: The Freedom Business, I told you about Profit First, Mike Michalowicz's system I use to organize the money that comes into my business, which he teaches in detail in his book *Profit First*. I have been implementing Profit First strategies ever since the day Lisa brought to my attention that no, I did not pay myself a salary.

What I now realize is that not paying myself a salary and not paying myself before I paid anyone else was one of the most unloving and disempowering things I've ever done to myself. If this is what you are currently doing to yourself, I would like you to seriously stop it now. If you are bringing in *any* level of income, then you *are* able to pay yourself. I don't care if it is $300 a month; you are, from this moment on, going to pay yourself a salary. Deal?

Here's the basic equation for determining your salary:

- Figure out the amount of money coming into your business

on a regular basis. Each business is unique in how it receives income. For example, I receive income twice a month, but your business might receive income monthly or quarterly. What is that number, generally speaking?

- With that number in mind, you then figure out your percentages. Example: if every two weeks, $1,500 comes into your business, then you take $1,500 and divide it up into the following percentage buckets:
  - **30 percent** of $1,500—$450 goes to your salary twice per month
  - **15 percent** of $1,500—$225 goes to your taxes twice per month
  - **55 percent** of $1,500—$825 goes to operating your business twice per month
- Or here is another example, using a business that generates $30,000 a month on average. The percentage buckets would look like this:
  - **30 percent** of $30,000—$9,000 goes to your salary each month
  - **15 percent** of $30,000—$4,500 goes to your taxes each month
  - **55 percent** of $30,000—$16,500 goes to operating your business each month

These are simplified versions of what these allocations can look like, and I encourage you to consider hiring a Profit First bookkeeper (yes, they exist). Visit the Profit First website, https://mikemichalowicz.com/profit-first/, to learn more.

One of the best parts of this approach is that you always have money put away to pay your taxes. (Did you just take a deep stress-relieving breath?) Having money put away to pay your taxes is, all by itself, enough to make this system *a must do.* Just imagine not having to scramble or worry about how you're going to pay your estimated taxes every three months. Instead, imagine this: it's tax time, and you go to your separate tax bank account and simply pay your taxes because the money is saved there. Then you go out for a fun lunch with a friend to celebrate. That is pretty darn close to an ecstatic experience.

That is the perfect lead-in to the other reason paying yourself first is essential: it's going to make you feel good, and feeling good is part of the freedom you want—freedom to feel relaxed, optimistic, enthusiastic, satisfied, peaceful, and other fabulous states of being that are important to you. On the flip side, there is truly nothing worse than working your butt off and not getting paid for it. Trudy Wilson, owner of a Mexican restaurant franchise, told me that during the economic crisis of 2020 brought on by the pandemic, she didn't pay herself at all, even though her business did bring in some money. She felt that paying her employees was the only priority at that time. This is the fastest way to compromise or damage your mental health. Even though it didn't make logical sense to pay herself when her business was suffering, in actuality, it would have been the best thing Trudy could do because paying herself is an act of self-love and appreciation for her efforts.

When you love and appreciate yourself for the work you do, more love and appreciation will come back to you in the form of money. I would never dream of not paying myself now, even if it is the tiniest amount. I know that taking away my salary is truly the worst thing I can do for my mindset, my well-being, and the growth of my business.

GETTING INTIMATE WITH YOUR INCOME STATEMENT

When I first started my business, you should have seen my bookkeeping. I had a lined ledger notebook (not online), and I would physically write down my income and the expenses. Very old-school. At the end of each quarter, I would go to my bank account and hope the number was the same as what was written in my notebook. Sometimes I would hit the jackpot, and my bank balance would be significantly over what I thought should be there. Yay! I've been as much as $4,000 over. But I've also been $4,000 under. Boo! At that time, I never quite understood what I did wrong and why my balance was frequently not the same as what I thought it should be. This ambiguity is a great example of how not to handle your books.

One day, Lisa said to me, "You really need to get a good book-keeper, Leslie." I will tell you the same thing right now. If you don't yet have a bookkeeper, make it a top priority. Hiring a professional bookkeeper is essential for your business. That bookkeeper needs to keep your books using an online system so you have access to those numbers whenever you want them. I use a bookkeeping system called Xero.

The income statement generated by having your books well-managed starts with two primary dollar amounts: the money that came in and the money that was spent. It also shows another critical figure, your net profit. Your net profit is the important stuff. It is the profit your business has made or hasn't made. As we spoke about in Chapter 2: The Freedom Business, we often get hung up on the sales number or what is often called our top line. Sometimes it can be disheartening to scroll down to the last section that says *net*. But that is where you need to look because that number tells you the true health of your business.

Most bookkeepers update your bookkeeping by the fifteenth of the next month. Make this a priority by scheduling into your calendar that each month on the fifteenth, you will review your income statement. In that way, you will be able to see in black-and-white what you are spending and if there are any expenses you can cut. By looking at your income statement each month, you will stay on top of and in control of your business finances.

YOUR BUSINESS SPEAKS

I love to cook, and unless it is a big holiday or a special dinner, I never use recipes. I do not use recipes because when I look at what is in my refrigerator, I find that the ingredients there speak to me, guide me, and tell me what to add. The basil says, "Choose me!" The chilis say, "We're here!" The garbanzo beans jump up and say, "We're exactly what you want!" When I listen to those ingredients and include them, my food is delicious.

In the same way meal ingredients speak to me, I have learned that my business speaks too—through numbers and income statements—and all I have to do is listen to what it is saying in order to stay on track. And, wow, it has a lot to say *all the time*. I know your business does too, unless you haven't yet launched it. Once you do, your opportunity to listen closely will come right away.

You are the captain of your business ship, and your job is to ensure that it gets where you want it to go. You do that by watching for its signals and listening to what it is telling you. The sinking of the great *Titanic* and the loss of many human beings happened because of the hubris of the operators and the owner. They were told about the iceberg, but they just did not listen because they couldn't see it or believe anything beyond their own ideas about the ship being unsinkable.

In order to listen to what your business is saying, you will often need to put preconceived ideas aside and be open to a shift in your own perception. Once you've received the input, then you can effectively take action.

There will come important thresholds where the message will be focused on expanding your offerings. No business can keep offering exactly the same products or services forever. If you do, you will get crushed from others who are keeping their offerings fresh or pivoting services to better help their clients. Expansion is the heart of a business, and to expand, you need to listen to what your business is telling you.

There are several ways your business speaks.

YOUR NUMBERS SPEAK

As we discussed before, your income statement is telling you whether your business is healthy or not, and whether you're making a profit or not. Those numbers don't lie, even though we wish they would sometimes. Looking at the numbers and seeing the reality is the conversation you want to be having with your business with great regularity.

YOUR PRODUCTS AND PROGRAMS SPEAK

My consultant, Lisa, has always told me, "Don't fall in love with your products." This is a juicy one. I have produced many dresses, sarongs, and sweaters that I personally loved but were total flops on Amazon. No matter how much you are in love with what you're selling—your product, program, digital course, training package, and so forth—it doesn't mean your customers will be. Even though you don't understand why in the world they didn't think your newest addition was the greatest thing since popcorn, it is your job as the business owner to recognize and acknowledge this and not defend it. The lack of sales is saying something to you. What is it? Is the price wrong? Is the color wrong? Is the design wrong? Is the program not offering enough substance and useful information? Are you offering it at the wrong time of year?

Just like your missteps and failures speak, as do your successes. For example, if one of my dresses sells well in black, I may expand the color offerings to add red and navy. If your coaching program did well, perhaps you can expand on it further or offer a shorter, condensed version of it in order to create another product out of it. You don't need to create something new all the time, but you can listen and look closely at your successes and expand on them.

YOUR CUSTOMERS SPEAK

In my early days of living in Europe, I was always surprised that business owners didn't adopt the American attitude of "the customer is always right." This was most apparent on the few occasions when I complained to a waiter about the food, and they became defensive and annoyed that I had expressed my dissatisfaction. That's a cultural quirk. But in the case of our customers in our businesses—yours and mine—we always need to be open to what they are saying to us. Way too often, we forget that without them, there is no business. Period.

The best thing you can do for your business is stay close to your customers and clients and regularly find out if they are happy with your services or products. The best ways to do this is to ask them by surveying them, writing to them, and best of all, calling them. Honestly and genuinely valuing your customers is the fastest way to gain raving fans. Remember, they will readily and happily tell you what they think of your whole operation if you ask.

Now take a big breath!

I know there is a lot to absorb in this chapter, and I've given you quite a lot to do. I promise if you make a practice of the activities and action steps recommended, you'll feel lighter because of them, not bogged down. Being awake and present with your business and your money will ultimately allow you to soar like an eagle—proud, wild, and free.

QUICK REVIEW

Taking action is critical. There are inner action steps and outer action steps, and both must be prioritized in order to create the business and life you want.

INNER ACTIONS RECAP:

- Intention-setting miracle where you write down your big vision and intentions
- Mirror miracle where you say your intention to yourself in the mirror
- Post-it miracle where you write your desired sales numbers on several Post-its

OUTER ACTIONS RECAP:

- Create to-do lists where you separate out personal and business tasks
- Prioritize the items on your daily list by asking, *What will make me the most money?*
- Schedule the tasks in your calendar
- Use the pomodoro technique for working in short bursts of time
- Create the big picture on a whiteboard (aka dry-erase board)
- Create your operations list
- Systemize your business by creating your SOPs, standard operating procedures
- Delegate and team-build
- Pay yourself first, and use the Profit First system
- Get a great online-based bookkeeper and online software tool
- Get intimate with your income statement (also called a profit and loss statement)
- Your business speaks. Listen to what it has to tell you about what's working, what's not working, and what to expand on.

WHERE WE'RE GOING NEXT

In the next chapter, you're going to receive Key #6 from which I believe you will derive great peace and strength. That said, what you are about to read might surprise you. So turn the page to find out what's in store.

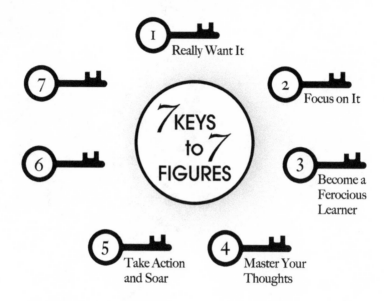

Chapter 9

KEY #6: GET USED TO SETBACKS AND FAILURES

"Fearlessness is not the absence of fear. It's the mastery of fear. It's about getting up one more time than we fall down."
—ARIANNA HUFFINGTON

There is a famous line in Bette Davis's classic 1950 Hollywood film *All about Eve* when she says in her inimitable style, "Fasten your seat belts; it's going to be a bumpy night." And, beautiful woman, that is how having your own business is from time to time—it can be very bumpy. Even with your best efforts, facets of your business will not always go as you want. You might lose a big customer or client, online product sales might drop, an email campaign might yield little results, expenses can explode, a high-profile interview might not result in the social media uptick you expected, and you might rather hide under the covers for a few days, *thank you very much*. Welcome to the life of an entrepreneur!

This is why, from the beginning of this book, I've been restating how critical it is for you to have a strong wanting. It is your wanting, your burning desire, and your yearning for something more than what you have now that will sustain you through the inevitable times of setbacks, failures, and the doubts that accompany them. Getting past them so they do not stop you—*by knowing how to get past them and choosing to do so*—is one of the greatest secrets to success. In fact, I see it as more of a skill than a secret, one I'm here to help you become good at.

As an entrepreneur you will be given challenges over and over again. Some of them will make you question if you should go on, some of them will force you to go into a new direction (such as creating a new product line or letting go of employees), and some of them might force you to start all over again. But there is one thing all challenges will do: they will test your resilience. It is resilience—your ability to stay in the game and persevere during difficult times—that will determine and fuel your success.

Do you want to know some of the challenges I've faced in my business? I have:

- Paid for all of the costs of a huge wholesale order from a large department store, which the store then canceled.
- Had hundreds of units of my merchandise stolen from a corrupt customs agenting company.
- Received no orders from buyers at a large trade show I invested a lot of money into.
- Almost closed my business during the 2008 global financial crisis because "it wasn't working."

- Had Amazon shut down all of my product listings because of a computer bot.
- Experienced plummeting sales during segments of 2020 and 2021 when the COVID-19 pandemic was rampant.
- Had a competitor copy my most popular designs.
- Had unethical sellers on Amazon steal my product page listings and undercut my prices.
- Had a warehouse reduce my storage space significantly so that I could not send in any new inventory and was sold out of bestsellers, forcing me to donate literally thousands of units of inventory so that I had more storage space *and* get another warehouse.

Shall I go on? I could, but I think you get the picture. Yes, I was tempted to throw in the towel on certain occasions, but as author Gena Showalter said, "Giving up is the only sure way to fail."

SUCCESSFUL PEOPLE ARE THE BIGGEST FAILURES OF ALL

I know that looking from the outside in, the lives of entrepreneurs who have "made it" can be discouraging, perhaps giving rise to the distressing feeling that success is beyond your grasp. But please keep in mind that the highly curated Instagram version of entrepreneurial bliss is just that—a carefully crafted image. The truth behind building our brands and businesses is usually messier and slower than social media standards would appreciate. Old-time Hollywood comedian Eddie Cantor wisely said, "It takes twenty years to become an overnight success." From the time I first started importing clothing to the time I hit the high six figures was a span of seventeen years!

(Unlike you, I didn't have this book in my hands to guide me, and so it will not take you that long.)

Another truth is that those who have "made it" have done so by persevering through failures and challenges, sometimes over many years. They found the courage to never give up even though they may have wanted to sometimes.

Do you know the story behind Sara Blakely's phenomenal success? Sara is the creator of Spanx, the shapewear brand and is the youngest self-made billionaire according to *Forbes*. Blakely failed her LSATs twice and ended up selling fax machines door to door for seven years. She openly shares that before the success of Spanx, her life was one big failure for the ten previous years. Then, on one auspicious day, she had an idea to cut off the legs of her pantyhose so she could wear them under her pants to make her butt look good. She had a great idea for a new product, but still, success did not come overnight. Sara was hard-pressed to find a manufacturer that would take her seriously and endured numerous rejections. But she persevered.

J. K. Rowling, the celebrated author of the *Harry Potter* book series, has a similar rags-to-riches story. Before the stupendous success of *Harry Potter*, which was rejected *twelve* times by publishers, J. K. was a jobless single mother living off unemployment benefits. She experienced years of financial difficulties, scraping by on welfare benefits and falling into depression for a period of time. She is now the richest author in the world.

Did you know that one of Oprah Winfrey's first jobs in TV ended abruptly after the producer declared she was "unfit for television"? Or that Walt Disney was fired from the *Kansas City*

Star newspaper because his editor felt he "lacked imagination and had no good ideas"? Or that Colonel Sanders of Kentucky Fried Chicken first pitched his restaurant idea at the age of sixty-two and was rejected, some say, 1,009 times?

Each one of these heroes gives us reason to redefine failure and reimagine its purpose in our lives.

NO CAN MEAN YES

As you're building your business, just know if it hasn't yet worked, that doesn't mean it won't work. One of my father's other favorite sayings was "No means yes." He always said the first no you receive just means you have to try harder to turn it into a yes, and he had an incredible experience to prove this. When my father was just starting out in a career and was newly married to my mom, he applied to Merrill Lynch's stockbroker training program. The big day finally came when the anticipated letter from Merrill Lynch arrived in the mailbox—the notification that would let him know if he was accepted into the program. He carefully opened the letter and, to his deep disappointment, read that they were terribly sorry, but he was not accepted. He was despondent, but my mother, who is the original *no means yes* believer, said to him, "You have to call them and find out why you were not accepted. Don't just accept this as final." She pushed him to get on the phone to Mr. Marcher, the man who had signed the letter, and find out the reason he was rejected. Well, guess what? He found out they had sent him the *wrong letter* by accident! Mr. Marcher was as surprised as my dad to find this out. An assistant had simply (and carelessly) sent out the rejection letter instead of the acceptance letter. If my mother hadn't pushed him to follow up, he would have walked away in defeat and never been in the training program. What a lesson! Sometimes, just one more phone call, email, pitch, or reminder will do the trick to land your first sale or whatever it is you are after—because no doesn't necessarily mean what we think it does.

PUMPING THE WATER

Have you ever seen those manual water pumps in a movie? A hunky, outdoorsy kind of guy walks over to his water pump on his ranch and starts pumping the water. His strong arms pump and pump and pump the old lever, but the water is deep down into the earth. He pumps more and more and still nothing comes. But he doesn't give up. He knows the water is there, and he just has to keep pumping and trying harder. Sure, his arms are sore and it's getting late, but he keeps pumping. And then, a trickle comes. The water starts to spurt out—spurt, stop, spurt—and the trickle turns into a stream and the stream turns into a gush. And all of a sudden, the water is coming out fast for our rugged friend, and his buckets are overflowing with gorgeous fresh water.

That's what you need to do with your business—you need to keep pumping the well until that liquid gold starts to flow. And yet *that*, right there, is the challenging part for all of us at times. It can be hard to have faith that the combination of our actions and our positive mindset is having the impact we intend when we aren't yet seeing the tangible results—like the deposits of money into our bank accounts, the increased traffic to our websites, or our social media followers growing in number. It's easy to get discouraged and to think the well is dry. It's helpful to know this stage of the process is normal.

All businesses go through it. It is precisely during this time that we need to persevere, even when there are few signposts pointing toward success and no guarantees. We need to draw on our inner resilience. We need to trust our instincts around which activities to prioritize, which creative ideas or solutions may carry us through adversity, how to pivot if necessary, and so forth. In short, we need to keep moving forward even when we're not seeing any evidence that we're getting anywhere.

In Ryan Daniel Moran's excellent book I already recommended, *12 Months to $1 Million*, he appropriately calls the time spent working on your business without seeing results "the grind." According to Ryan, all businesses go through three stages: the grind, the growth, and the gold. Understanding this will help you keep going when no one is liking or commenting on your posts, or subscribing to your videos, or buying your product or service. Just know this is part of the entrepreneurial deal. But "the grind" won't go on forever, and your perseverance will carry you through it.

During the many years when my business was hovering below $50,000 in yearly revenue, I often had a mental image of my business as a large boulder. In my mind, I saw myself pushing the boulder up a hill with all my might. I had two hands on the boulder, digging my heels into the ground so I wouldn't fall back, and with each push, I would take another small step forward. The boulder was heavy, but I kept pushing and pushing. I knew once I could get the boulder to the top of the hill, it would start to roll down the other side effortlessly. Then one day, that's exactly what happened. The boulder started to roll gracefully down the other side—past the grind. I metaphorically pushed my business up the hill by wanting it, focusing on it, becoming a ferocious learner, keeping my thoughts positive, and taking the action steps needed before seeing results—all until the work I had done started to pay off and things started to flow without as much effort. The results finally showed up the following year when my business grew from $50,000 to $100,000 in annual revenue. By then, I had a lot more "muscle mass" in my mind and heart from pushing that business boulder up the hill. I was stronger in every way.

OUR CHALLENGES ARE OUR GREATEST TEACHERS

The challenges we are given turn out to be the grist for the mill that builds up our character, and character gives us the raw materials we need to build up our resilience. Integrity, honor, courage, compassion—these are just a few of the other facets of character that deepen and grow. With strength of character, we're able to go forward with trust and faith, even when we are faced with great difficulties in our business or in our personal life.

And as you may have experienced yourself, sometimes our character-building challenges happen far too early.

When I was seventeen years old, I fell in love with a beautiful boy with long blond hair whose name was Andy. Andy was my first love. He was kind and always good to me, even visiting me when I was sick in bed, bringing me a small gift to lift my spirits. My high school graduation day came, and the icing on the cake was the romantic celebration dinner I had to look forward to. Andy was excited too. To pick me up for our special dinner, he was driving from Rutgers University in New Jersey to West Orange, the New Jersey town where I lived. Except he never arrived.

Andy died in a car accident on his way to pick me up. He was nineteen years old.

At the young age of seventeen, I was shaken from my childhood years into the reality of death; not a typical experience for a teenager to have, at least not where I grew up in the New Jersey suburbs. For the first year after Andy's death, I was essentially in a state of shock, grief, and sadness. But even so, there was something else growing inside of me. In those tender years, a thought came over me and never left. When it first emerged, I was sitting with my mom in a restaurant in New York City, and I said to her, "Difficult things happen, but it is what we *do* with those difficult experiences that count. They can either bring us down or lift us up." I'm not sure where that spark of wisdom came from at my young age, but I knew I had the power of choice, and the kind of choices I would make during the hard times would be defining moments. They would shape me. I came to understand that the tragic experience of losing Andy could make me a victim or make me stronger. I chose stronger.

In many ways, that piece of wisdom has been *the* gift that has helped me deal with many more challenges that came after this turning point at seventeen—some of which you know from earlier chapters. All experiences of loss, hardship, setbacks, or down-right failures, if looked at with the intention to learn and grow from them, can be your greatest teachers and catalysts. And they can lead directly to the success of your business. They can give you great perspective and fuel you with determination and clarity of direction.

"Expect future obstacles and difficulties," says Dr. David Schwartz, author of *The Magic of Thinking Big*. "Every venture presents risks, problems, and uncertainties. Just know they are going to be coming," he asserts. When we know this and realize it's a part of every entrepreneur's experience, and not just ours alone, it gives us more courage to go on. This is why I believe that being an entrepreneur is a path toward self-transformation. The very nature of the entrepreneurial spirit is to take initiative and take big risks, which requires us to learn and grow and persevere over and over again.

Our challenges push us in new directions. These new directions can cause us to take action steps we never would have taken without first having the challenge. Here are a few examples:

- When I had problems on Amazon, it forced me to create my own website and to grow a customer email list, which gave me other ways to expand my business.
- When Arlene, who owned a restaurant, could only offer takeout due to the global pandemic, she created an online soup delivery business. This specialized menu gave her another income stream that previously did not exist.
- When Beth, owner of a wholesale clothing company, lost her biggest wholesale customer (which was 80 percent of her revenue), it forced her to create her own website, stop wholesaling altogether, and pivot to a retail business, selling directly to customers.
- When Tracy of Party Artistry, an event planning company, had to shut down because large parties weren't happen-

ing, it gave her the opportunity to focus on activities that would help her company rocket forward once big events were allowed again. This included networking to drum up new potential clients, reviewing all facets of her operation, getting super organized, and building a stronger social media presence.

- When Sonya lost her ability to hold large in-person events—which she had offered around the world—she was suddenly forced to stay home. Not only did she get the rest she needed, but she also learned to sell online so she could make money from anywhere, anytime.

The next time challenges come your way—and they will—remember that they may be pushing you in an even better direction.

FEAR OF FAILURE

When my first husband and I divorced, my ex-mother-in-law said to me, "Your marriage was a failure." The statement startled me, as I didn't see it that way. Sure, the marriage didn't last, but the relationship, which also included wonderful experiences, was no failure in my eyes. Then as now, I look at it as an experience in my life that brought me to where I am, and without it, I would not be the person I am, now living happily with my husband, Heinz. In fact, I choose to never think of any experience as a failure, whether it is positive or negative. So-called failures are just learning experiences. The only real failure you can have is to not learn anything from your so-called failures.

I love Thomas Edison's view of failure. He said, "I have not failed. I've just found ten thousand ways that won't work." Of course, he was talking about the ten thousand times he "failed" at perfecting the incandescent electric light bulb. Just think, we might be still reading by gaslight if he hadn't *failed* so many times. Thank goodness for his failures.

Author Paulo Coelho said, "There is only one thing that makes a dream impossible to achieve: the fear of failure." While writing this book, I surveyed many women entrepreneurs about their challenges as business owners. What came up over and over was their struggle with fear. Can you relate to any of the following fears?

- Fear of being judged
- Fear of not being good enough
- Fear of not knowing how to use and manage the technology and systems you need to run your business
- Fear of not knowing how to help your clients or customers
- Fear you won't ever make the money you want
- Fear you will lose the money once you make it
- Fear you will lose your relationship if you become successful

Not only do we have to deal with our own fears (if that weren't quite enough); we have to deal with other people's fears too. What would your husband, partner, father, mother, friend, or _____ (fill in the blank) think if you were to choose to do some (or all) of the following?

- Start your own business
- Use money you don't have to hire a consultant or coach
- Quit your job to follow a dream
- Hire childcare so you can get work done
- Become an empowered, independent entrepreneur

- Choose to be highly visible on social media and become widely known
- Earn more than anyone else ever did in your family
- Have an abundance of money and other resources at your fingertips at all times

How do we move beyond these real fears that slow down our growth and sometimes paralyze us? How can we reclaim the power that we give to these kinds of fears and render them harmless? Read on.

THE #1 GUARANTEED CURE FOR FEAR

Facing our fears is both an internal and external job. Meditating, praying, deep breathing, connecting with our higher self, and taking long walks in nature certainly help to give us perspective and strength. But I have found that the fear-busting results from inner work are not long-lasting. The noise of the world is too overbearing. Based on my own experience and the results I've witnessed with my clients, there is one way to overcome fear that is more potent than any other.

TAKE ACTION

Having just read Chapter 8, you already know I'm a cheerleader for taking action. It is Key #5 for creating your seven-figure business and life, after all. The fact that it can cure fear is an indicator of how profound taking action can be when done with clarity, intention, passion, and commitment.

It cures fear because the action you take—such as renting an office, or announcing your course, or getting samples of a new product—will give you tangible results. You may start your coaching or consulting practice, enroll your first course participant, or get your first online sale. Those accomplishments are what will melt away the fear like hot sizzling butter in a pan, guaranteed. Confidence is not achieved within your mind; confidence is the result of taking action and seeing the results of that action.

In *The Magic of Thinking Big*, Dr. Schwartz also says, "Action feeds and strengthens confidence, inaction in all forms feeds fear. To fight fear, act. To increase fear—wait, put off, postpone." This sage advice represents the razor's edge. We've all had the experience of something seeming much scarier before we actually do it. The idea of traveling by myself when I first went to Indonesia was petrifying, but once on the plane, the fear dissolved. Giving my first speech in Toast Masters was so scary, until I got in front of the room and started talking. Hiring my first assistant was anxiety-provoking, until I did it and discovered how much I love having the help.

How about you? Think about some things you were truly afraid of doing, and then, once you did them, something shifted inside you. You felt lighter. Stronger. Freer.

> *"Let me assert my firm belief that the only thing we have to fear is fear itself—nameless, unreasoning, unjustified terror which paralyzes needed efforts to convert retreat into advance."*
>
> —FRANKLIN D. ROOSEVELT

OH, THOSE SABOTAGING ATTITUDES AND BEHAVIORS

When we let difficult circumstances, setbacks, and failures join forces with our fears, the inner flame of our hunger for expansion and evolution can be severely compromised. That beautiful flame can even get snuffed out. In a panic (usually a quiet, seemingly dignified panic), we roll out the red carpet for sabotaging thoughts, attitudes, and behaviors. In other words, when we're not taking conscious action and consciously choosing how we want to view our circumstances, unconscious behaviors and beliefs can fill the void. Let's look at some of the most common saboteurs women entrepreneurs face.

SABOTEUR #1: WHY BOTHER?

Taking risks and putting yourself out there is not comfortable. That is, of course, an understatement! It can feel debilitating and terrifying. The first time I posted one of my videos on YouTube, I was petrified. I understand that getting out of our comfort zone is *hard*. And there are countless reasons, justifications, and excuses we can draw on to ensure we remain in our comfort zone. Asking "Why bother?" may be one of the easiest rationales of all. When you find yourself questioning why you are working so hard on your dream or why you're putting up with so much uncertainty, do you overhear yourself making statements (thinly disguised as legitimate questions) like the following:

- Why bother building an Instagram following?
- Why bother making videos?
- Why bother starting an e-commerce business?
- Why bother using savings to pay for a coach or a training program?
- Why bother going through the steps to launch a course?
- Why bother risking my job (which pays the bills) to step into the unknown?

- Why bother leaving my princess tower? It's so comfy here. (Remember the tower from Chapter 3?)

"Why bother?" is a top sabotaging attitude for many of us women, at least on occasion. So let's look at this one dead-on because there is much more at stake than our comfort zones. What we can feel inside that "why bother?" is a dangerous combination of fear, resistance, and resignation—and usually with some anger mixed in. Disillusionment and despair aren't far behind if we hang on to "why bother?" for too long. And, beautiful woman, that downward pathway isn't for you. I know this about you without ever having met you in person. You were born for greatness, not cynicism.

SABOTEUR #2: INDECISION

Don't you hate it when you can't decide on something? It is such a waste of time and is emotionally draining too. *Should I? Shouldn't I?* This wavering stops us dead in our tracks rather than allowing us to enjoy the momentum that taking action offers. In his classic book *Think and Grow Rich*, Napoleon Hill says, "Accurate analysis of over 25,000 people who had experienced failure disclosed the fact that 'lack of decision' was near the head of the list of the thirty major causes of failure." He goes on to say that those who have accumulated wealth have the habit of reaching decisions quickly. Over time, I have come to love making decisions and sticking to them. The gifts that decisiveness gives us are similar to those that perseverance gives us, starting with self-trust and self-respect. Those are like the finest gold. When we're not holding ourselves hostage through indecision, energy and vitality are unleashed. It's also worth remembering that not making a decision is actually a decision too—to *not* do something.

SABOTEUR #3: OVERWHELM

If you had a dollar for every time you've said, "I am so over-whelmed!" how wealthy would you be? While teaching my online course Keys to Success, overwhelm was by far one of the biggest challenges the women participating faced. "I'm so overwhelmed, I don't know what to do first" was the primary reason I decided to offer the course in the first place. For women entrepreneurs, overwhelm is an epidemic. It happens because when you are the CEO of your own enterprise, there are many different tasks that need to be done in order to keep the ship sailing smoothly. What do you do first? What could be an easy question to answer becomes stressful when overwhelm has zapped you of your focus, concentration, clarity, and inspiration. When this happens, turn your attention to ground zero: get crystal clear on your intentions and write down the action steps that are fully aligned with them, just as we discussed in the previous chapter. And remember that you don't have to take all steps simultaneously, nor will you want to. Use this as an opportunity to practice taking action in a way, and at a pace, that feels good.

When I trained with Lisa Nichols in her course Speaking and Inspiring, she said something that forever changed my relationship with the O-word: "Overwhelm is a choice." That one got me. The truth of it rang like a Zen master's bell, reminding me that every time we consciously make a new, healthy choice, we are owning our power.

SABOTEUR #4: PERFECTIONISM

Do you find yourself ceaselessly tending to the details of your existing business, or the one you're in the early stages of developing, and taking a *long* time to meet your big goals? Are you forever tweaking your website, or reshooting videos, or rethinking your digital course content, or researching your competitors' products and services, or interviewing your fifteenth virtual assistant candidate, or enrolling in another training program on how to be successful in your industry? Although each of these tasks matters, overfocusing on getting it all "just right" can be a form of procrastination. And I have to say, procrastination and perfectionism are totally made for each other! While we're busy tinkering and perseverating, the sales aren't coming in like they could be because we haven't opened the doors and let the world in. Sometimes we simply have to take the leap! Post the video that starts with our eyes closed or put the product online even though the photos are not as good as they could be. When I look back at my Amazon product pages from when I first started, I can see that they were awful. The copywriting was bad and any inclusion of keywords for search engine optimization was accidental. My photos were terrible. The pages were *not* marketing gold. But here's the thing—they were up and running, product was for sale, and money was coming in. Fine-tuning, as it turned out, could come later.

How many podcasts will you listen to or how many training videos will you watch before you give yourself the green light to go? Sometimes we just have to call it "good enough for now" and press send with our imperfect work. Making a habit of doing this is also astoundingly helpful for moving through challenging periods in your business.

SABOTEUR #5: DOUBT

Can I? Should I? Is it the right time? Should I wait? Is this what I should be doing? How can I possibly get noticed with so many others shouting from the rooftops? There are periods of time when we all suffer from this most insidious disease called doubt. Often, doubt is tied to our issues of worthiness and "enoughness." The voice of doubt sadly asks, *Am I good enough, smart enough, different enough, or special enough to run this business, teach this body of work, or be a leader in my field? Maybe I'm just an impostor who will be found out and humiliated.* Guess what? Even if all of that were true (and it isn't), it doesn't matter. The goal is not to be the greatest, the best, the supreme leader of all. The goal is to have a business that serves you, that is aligned with your authentic success, and that gives you the money and freedom you want. And just like dealing with indecision and perfectionism, the best way to combat doubt is to "just do it." Action will take you where doubt would never have the guts to go.

JUST KEEP GOING

It is normal to be doubtful, it is normal to question what you are doing, and yes, it's normal to be afraid and fall into self-sabotaging behaviors and thoughts. I want to normalize all of this for you. In addition to being normal aspects of taking risks as a self-made business owner, it all just comes with the territory of being human. However, being an entrepreneur is much, much more than an exercise in overcoming obstacles and fears. Built right into our entrepreneurial DNA is an antidote to the fear, a wondrous superpower: *the power is having no idea what you are doing at times and doing it anyway.* You are the boss. You are the queen. You are the hero of your own story—in business and beyond.

You *do it anyway* because you are on a mission. Some of us have a mission to help others with our products or services, some of us have a mission to have more family time, some of us want to only answer to ourselves, some of us want to make big bucks, and some of us want all of those things and then some. Whatever your mission is, it is a great treasure because it will keep you going forward even when you've stumbled or fallen in some way. It will be the reason to pick yourself up again. If there comes a time when your mission needs to change course and be expressed in new ways, you will have a clear and deep knowing of it and recognize it as the truth. As my mentor Ali Brown says, you may need to "take a sharp right turn" and create a new product line, or change your sales strategy, or bring your brick-and-mortar business completely online.

Whether you're at the early stages of dreaming and conceptualizing your business or you're already well established, don't underestimate the power of just *staying in the game of business.* What would have happened if Sara Blakely from Spanx had given up when she had trouble finding a manufacturer that would work with her, or if J. K. Rowling had stopped submitting her book to publishers? I know for sure that my own perseverance—the fact that I just kept my business going over the years no matter what—is one of the reasons for the success that I now enjoy.

> "I had the happy privilege of analyzing both Mr. Edison and Mr. Ford, year by year, over a long period of years, and therefore, the opportunity to study them at close range, so I speak from actual knowledge when I say that I found no quality save persistence, in either of them, that even remotely suggested the major source of their stupendous achievements."
>
> —NAPOLEON HILL IN *THINK AND GROW RICH*

THE GOAL IS NOT THE POINT

What happens when you don't reach a sales goal you have painstakingly focused on for months and months? What do you do? Wrestling with setbacks and failures is usually tied to not reaching certain goals we've set for ourselves. We may overspend on the way to achieving them, or we go through too much stress, and things simply don't work out.

Brooke Castillo, the supercoach I introduced you to earlier, has a lot to say about not reaching goals. She says that reaching the exact goal we've set for ourselves is actually not the point. The point, rather, is the *process*, not the results. More specifically, the point is who you are becoming while you are reaching for the goals. The point is the growth and adventure you experience on your journey of becoming a woman of ever-expanding vision, knowledge, creativity, contribution, confidence, resilience, gratitude, abundance, freedom, and joy.

The next time you're faced with a challenge or what appears to be a major setback, remember that no situation or circumstance is bigger than *you*. You might even thank that setback one day. Your setbacks and failures are the catalysts to bring you along your path of success.

FOUR STEPS FOR MOVING FORWARD

1. You might be saying, "But, Leslie, I feel stuck. I don't have the time or money I need to get more time and money. Help!" If you don't have enough money to take action, don't have a lot of extra time, and don't have enough (or any) outside support, here are four steps to consider taking right away. You won't be surprised to know that the first step is to

get in touch with your wanting and yearning. When you're feeling scared, I know this may seem next to impossible. This is where I want to encourage you to muster up a little faith in your own inner flame, even if it's a small flicker at the moment. It's always been smoldering away within you, and I'm sure you've relied on it to move through other challenging times in your life. Turn toward it again now so you can remember your passion for living, growing, and evolving. In truth, this passion is much bigger than your fear (even if it doesn't feel like it right now). Lean into it.

2. Remind yourself that if you don't make changes now, you are going to be in exactly the same situation one year from now. Let that reality sink in. The time is now. Can you afford to wait any longer?

3. Take some concrete actions toward bringing in extra money. Can you cut back on expenses and start saving a portion of your income? Can you take on any side hustles to make extra cash? For example, is there something you can teach or offer on a consulting or subcontracting basis such as creating a website, mastering Facebook ads, or selling used items at an outdoor market? There are several freelance platforms online where you can offer your services such as Upwork, Freelancer, Fiverr, and 99 Designs, delivering services like photoshopping, graphic design, copywriting, video editing, or virtual assistant support.

4. With the extra money that you save, create on the side, or both, invest in trainings that will put money in your pocket. For example, that training that teaches you how to sell an online course is going to literally put money in your pocket if you do the work. That consultant who knows how to launch an e-commerce business is going to teach you how to make sales. The money you earn now should go into resources that will give you a return on your investment (ROI).

If you feel there is no way to cut back on expenses to save more or you have no time for any side hustle, then you need to find the information online. The reason to pay for courses or to hire consultants is because it's usually a quicker path to reach your goals and you get your hand held through the process. But that same information is available to everyone for free on the internet if you have the motivation to find it, learn it, and take action on it.

I sincerely believe when your yearning, wanting, and will are strong enough, you will find a way. Even though it may not be easy, it *is* possible. Once you decide and take action, the universe will be there to support you, and that is more than a quaint New Age saying. It is simply true.

QUICK REVIEW

You are almost there. You now have six of the 7 Keys to money and freedom in your hands. Let's recap.

- Key #1: Really Want It
- Key #2: Focus on It
- Key #3: Become a Ferocious Learner
- Key #4: Master Your Thoughts
- Key #5: Take Action and Soar
- Key #6: Get Used to Setbacks and Failures

WHERE WE'RE GOING NEXT

Turn the page to claim the power of Key #7—the final key that may surprise you in the best way.

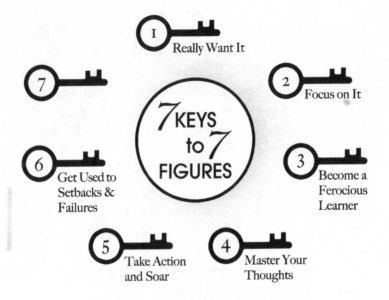

Chapter 10

KEY #7: EMBRACE NON-DOING

*"Emptiness is not really empty; emptiness is full of
everything. The 'everything' just isn't manifest."*
—RAM DASS

Here is a radical thought for you: if you want to be successful
in business, you need to stop doing business. That might sound
contradictory, but it isn't. The deep secret behind phenomenal
success lies in taking time in your life to non-do and to become
empty. It is by making time for emptiness in your life that you
and your business will flourish.

The natural world is a testament to this statement. Every animal
instinctively knows there are times to rest and times to be
active. Nature flourishes with the rhythms of both night and
day, sunshine and clouds. Farmland fields are allowed to lie
fallow for a few seasons so the soil can rest and regenerate. We
humans also have natural rhythms and needs, and when we
follow them, we thrive. The trouble is, we've gotten out of touch

with our essential nature. We often think we have no time to pay attention to our natural rhythms or to "indulge" in self-care, but the truth is when you make them a priority, they will come together as one of your greatest powers—a nourishing power.

I knew nothing about the importance of empty time in my early thirties. Sure, I had heard about meditation and spirituality, but I felt it wasn't really for me. It all just seemed too weird, like something for New Agers and hippy-dippy people. At that time, I was more interested in my then-marriage, figuring out my career path, and getting pregnant. But life had other plans. Life is a formidable teacher. It keeps giving us challenges that force us to grow and change and often to change course, whether we want to or not.

Life's other plan came in the form of my first miscarriage. The pain of a miscarriage is profound. Getting pregnant, experiencing the joy of the new life inside of you, imagining a future that includes your own family, and then experiencing your baby dying—there are no words, actually. If you have also experienced the pain of a miscarriage or miscarriages, my heart goes out to you, sister. Those of us who have experienced this loss understand how truly devastating it is.

In my case, I continued living life as it was, working in a public relations job I didn't like, and trying to get pregnant again. And it happened—I did get pregnant again! I felt so joyous and grateful and hopeful that this baby would live—until I miscarried for the second time. Soon thereafter, my then-husband had an opportunity for a job in Atlanta, and we decided to accept the offer. We moved there from New York City. I was still floundering in my career, and each moment of my day was spent worrying over whether I would get pregnant again and whether the baby would survive. I ate well, I rested, I went to my doctor appointments, and I hoped. For those of us who have experienced infertility, we know the obsession that this can become and the pain it causes.

Luckily, I did become pregnant again! I was so happy!

And then.

Not pregnant.

I experienced my third miscarriage.

I truly believe life keeps throwing us punches until we make the changes it is asking us to make. The first miscarriage came— boom—and I didn't change anything about the way I was living. Then life said, "Oh no, she's not getting it! Let's go for another punch." And boom, another miscarriage. "Nope, she still hasn't made any changes. We better go for the big bomb." Then boom, like a cannonball, the third miscarriage blasted me out of my marriage and landed me at a spiritual meditation retreat in New Mexico that my dad recommended.

TIME TO WAKE UP

I had no interest in anything spiritual at that time, as I mentioned, and I thought it was really "weird" that my dad sometimes went to a meditation retreat. But I was suffering so much from my losses that going somewhere to heal and rest was just what I needed. What's more, I had always loved New Mexico.

I couldn't get there quickly enough.

Once I was on my way, I became a river of tears. I cried while flying from Atlanta to Albuquerque; I cried when the retreat staff picked me up in their car; I cried during the workshop sessions. I cried for all the dreams I wanted to live that seemed so far out of reach right then. But after being there for a week, I noticed that I was starting to feel better. There were moments when I actually felt happy and contented and peaceful, even in the wake of three miscarriages, and the pain all of that caused. How was it possible to feel some joy during one of the worst times of my life? Yet, like tiny beams you see in the distance as a faraway car moves closer, there was a light inside of me that was starting to grow.

What was that light? There were lots of different possibilities and ways to define it. Was it the result of some much-needed rest and recuperation? Was it being surrounded by other people who were focused on healing and spiritual connection? Was it a more positive, optimistic mindset? Was it my higher self shining through? Was it the Divine?

Whatever the source may have been, all I can tell you is that week at the retreat made me feel like I woke up into a truly new world, like Dorothy when she landed in Oz. The colors of nature became more vibrant, my hearing became more vivid, my body opened up to dancing, and my heart exploded open with the poignancy of connecting with nature. Most of all, it was the experience of connecting with *something greater than myself* that was awe-inspiringly new for me. Much of what I thought I knew for certain paled when held up against this flourishing aliveness I had never felt before. It was bigger than anything my own thoughts could have created. Outside my normal experience, it felt like a deep connection to all of life and an inner knowing that everything was going to be okay. This had such a positive effect on me that—get this—every summer for over thirty years now, I have continued to go to that same retreat. Yep, over three decades.

Taking this dedicated time off, year after year, to quiet my mind, to empty out, and to connect more deeply with nature has nourished and supported every part of my life—my inner life as well as my business life. Taking time away from my business—stopping *to do business*—has had *no* adverse effects AT ALL! In fact, it is one of the greatest secrets to my success. I have been practicing Key #7 for decades, and I can tell you most assuredly that prioritizing empty time has resulted in having a successful business that continues to grow without me being constantly exhausted, stressed, and overworked. It is responsible for the kind of life I now have—one that is abundant in both money and freedom.

Another way to view this kind of empty time is to understand its power: it ushers us into a deeply feminine state of receptivity where we become open to *receiving* all the riches that life wants to lay at our feet. It softly invites us to surrender, opening the floodgates for things to flow *to* us rather than from us—creative ideas, insights, connections, and an ocean of possibilities and opportunities.

So yes, sometimes the absolute best thing we can do for our business, and our entrepreneurial goals and dreams, is to stop and do nothing. No-thing. Nada.

This is why it's paramount for you, beautiful woman, to create more empty space in your life—to become friends with the sacred void that is always pregnant with new possibilities. Rest and rejuvenation will sprout and nourish seeds of creativity and innovation within you that will blossom into your greatest success.

NON-DOING KEEPS YOU ON *YOUR* TRACK

As we discussed in Chapter 2, defining, pursuing, and attaining our own authentic success is one of the most important quests of a lifetime. But without taking time to be quiet, silent, and empty—without having downtime or non-doing time—it's hard to hear the still, small voice within that knows what authentic success really means to us. The only way to acquaint ourselves with our inner knowing voice is to make time in our lives to actually hear her.

Non-doing allows you to empty out so you can hear what your deepest yearnings are, which puts you in touch with your authentic success and keeps you on that track—*your track.* When you give yourself that non-doing time, you can connect with what you really want instead of going after things you *think* you want. As you probably know very well, when you get exhausted and are way too busy and overstretched and working long hours over an extended period of time, you can end up making choices that aren't truly what you want but that might seem like a way out. For example, I've watched women choose to shut down their businesses, take jobs they're not happy about, and even leave relationships. When you don't give yourself non-doing time—empty time—it's very difficult to truly *feel* or *know* what it is that you really, really, really want and yearn for. Without stopping to listen, you can find yourself living on a conveyer belt of actions that never really leads anywhere; it just goes round and round.

TEAMING UP WITH YOUR INNER GUIDANCE SYSTEM

Okay, I can hear what you are thinking.

"But *how* can I make more space in my life?" you ask. "I just don't see it."

That's understandable because when we fill every moment of our lives with doing and action, there really appears to be no space for anything new to come in. It's like having a drawer that is stuffed so full with clothing that you can't close it. You simply need to remove some items so the drawer is functional again. Or maybe you can relate more to eating way too much at Thanksgiving or another holiday and not having space for that slice of pumpkin pie...plus your mom's special cheesecake... and the sliver of pecan pie you were secretly looking forward to.

There is only one good answer when it comes to figuring out how to have more space in your life: you have to take it! You have to make it! You have to select the times and places when your own space is priority number one. It's scheduled and calendared. Taking control in this way is one of the best decisions you will ever make, primarily because it will allow you to hear your brilliant inner guidance.

Tony Robbins had a mentor who told him early on that success comes when you work on yourself as much as you work on your business. I love that! And look at how Tony is doing—not bad! Other phenomenally successful people have pointed to the inner world of the self as being of utmost importance. Albert Einstein said, "The only real valuable thing is intuition. The intuitive mind is a sacred gift." Steve Jobs echoed this when he said, "Intuition is a very powerful thing...more powerful than intellect, in my opinion."

As for the feminine voice, Oprah said, "I've trusted the still, small voice of intuition my entire life. And the only time I've made mistakes is when I didn't listen. For all the major moves in my life I've trusted my instincts."

It is in the empty space—where the mind is quiet, the heart is full, and the feeling of well-being is abundant—that we access our intuition and inner guidance. We are far more than the sum total of what we have learned or inherited. We are extraordinary beings who can tap into a deeper knowing that is far beyond our own personal learning or circumstances. We are all gifted with the ability to tap into something greater than ourselves, and that happens with greater ease when we allow ourselves to open—to be an empty vessel that is receptive to *life*.

Let's get real. Life can be really hard. Who hasn't had some heartbreaking challenges? No one. Consciously creating a pathway that leads you into the world of your inner knowing is essential; it's access to a precious, private place of peace that you can always go to. Your own slice of heaven while here on earth. Without that inner refuge, we are subject to the storms of life without the necessary protections that help us to keep perspective when times are hard.

There was a time when I would find myself consumed by concern and worry too easily and too often. *Suppose this happens, and sup-*

pose that happens, I would think to myself. But I can tell you with enthusiasm that the spiritual practices I've been devoted to over many years, like meditation, are some of my greatest gifts. They transport me out of my worries and problems quickly. I often meditate with Heinz, and it's like a bar of soap melting away in hot water—over the half hour, any worry that's plaguing me or my husband just starts to disappear. Why? Because we're able to access our natural state that is always there but can get covered up with unproductive thoughts. For any and all of us, perhaps the most powerful part of accessing our inner guidance—or inner being—is that we're tuning into the aspect of ourselves that has never forgotten its connection to the source of all things. This connection is one of the greatest joys and successes of a lifetime.

BLISS IS YOUR NATURAL STATE

While cozied up in our tent in New Mexico one summer, Heinz and I had an entertaining hour watching with amazement as a squirrel frolicked and played outside. Multiple times it ran up our tent and slid down the other side like a child on a playground. Up and down and all around it went—over and over and over— simply because it felt like having some fun. Joy is the natural state of all living things. Babies, puppies, dolphins, you, and me. That is who we really are. We are *made* for joy. What's more, when we connect with that state of joy and happiness and acknowledge that we have a higher self that is here to guide and help us, all aspects of our lives thrive, including our businesses. There is nothing like slowing things down and entering into empty time to put us directly in touch with this inner well of delight.

My friend Julie and I went traveling through Spain during our junior year in college, an experience I'll never forget. While walking down the street in Seville and munching on *turrón*, the famous Spanish candy, the words "void land" kept popping into my thoughts. Void land might sound like a twenty-year-old's desire to escape reality through an alcohol- or drug-induced stupor, but looking back, I think it was my soul reminding me of my natural state of peace. Right there on a sunny sidewalk in Spain, it chose the term "void land," which has continued for years to be one that I use when describing this special place of non-doing and emptiness.

We all yearn to be in void land, which is why we often try to get there with alcohol, drugs, or other experiences that turn out to be nowhere near as positive as our innate desire for peace. The truth is, we all kind of remember, consciously or unconsciously, that peace and emptiness are central to who we are. It's not something we have to become; it's an uncovering of what is already there. The Sufis, the spiritual mystics and philosophers of ancient Islam, refer to this as removing the many layers of veils. Experiencing non-doing and empty time is the most potent way to remove the veils in order to find peace.

Perhaps the thought of non-doing and having more mental and emotional space sounds great but also impossible for your life. You have work you do, children to take care of, and responsibilities that won't wait. But I must tell you that if you make this a non-negotiable priority, you will be blown away by the results. You will want to shout from the rooftops that you have uncovered one of life's best-kept secrets.

And there's more.

If you are willing to have the sheer audacity to make being content and happy your number one priority, everyone around you will benefit. Even if they can't put their finger on what they feel or sense around you, others will feel good in your presence. Your inner spaciousness will invite their inner spaciousness. Your inspiration will beckon theirs. You will be an oasis for others *and* for yourself. Think for a moment about what that means. Being an oasis is more than a pretty metaphor. It's *you* being a place of refreshment, rejuvenation, and pleasure right in the midst of the aridness of turbulent times.

Aristotle said, "Happiness is the meaning and the purpose of life, the whole aim and end of human existence." He was a pretty on-point guy, right? Loving yourself, feeling that your life is in a state of flow, connecting to your intuition, and connecting to the Divine will give rise to your happiness, aliveness, and your extraordinary dreams. Sure, you can live without these feelings and connections—sadly, most people do. But why not open your arms and say yes to this precious gift of being connected to your soul and spirit?

CAN WE ALL SAY YES TO BEING?

It is difficult to go against the grain and live in a way that is different from what most people think is the right way to live and to pursue success in unconventional ways. We are taught that success comes as a result of working hard, being busy, and pushing toward our goals.

Push, push, push. Do, do, do. More, more, more.

Aren't we all a bit tired of this? Aren't *you* tired of this?

Let's stop for a second and take this in: *Aren't we women tired of this?*

Let's imagine we are all together right now in an elegant workshop room overlooking the sea. Filled with a beautiful determination, we stand up, throw open the windows, and shout in unison:

"YEESSSS, we are tired of this!"

But wait. That's not all. "We're also exhausted, discouraged, disenchanted, uninspired, and sometimes horribly depressed. We want to stop the madness and change our lives!"

I want you to know that I understand, and I know you *can* change your life. That's why I wrote this book—not only so you can create more money and enjoy the freedom you've always wanted, but so you can achieve your goals without constantly pushing yourself into states of unmanageable stress, tension, fatigue, and burnout.

Creating goals and following the steps to get there is one way to achievement, but it is not the *only* way. There is an easier way to get there: by putting yourself in a natural state of well-being and contentment. It's a feminine approach to getting what you want. It's a more receptive way to achieve. You know you're tapping into your feminine essence strengths when you're:

- Relaxed and calm
- Aware of what your intuition is telling you
- In touch with what you feel
- Attuned to your imagination

- Aware of your deeper yearnings
- Trusting good things will come to you
- Open to wonder
- And knowing you don't have to figure it all out

The masculine approach is more about *pushing* toward goals; the feminine approach is more about getting clear on our deepest yearnings and *pulling* those yearnings toward us. According to the feminine approach, we manifest best when we are in a state of openness and willingness, not in a state of striving and straining. "The power to manifest comes from *well-being* not just from doing," says Dr. Claire Zammit.

The *pulling* approach is how Trevor G. Blake created a business that sold for over $100 million. In his book, *Three Simple Steps: A Map to Success in Business and Life*, he says entrepreneurs should be more like a wizard (feminine) than a warrior (masculine). He says, "All you need to do is set an intention, then relax and let life fill in the details. There is no point to trying to conquer the goal in the warrior style by charging toward the treasure. For all you know, you could be running in the wrong direction. Be like a wizard. The intention is your magic spell."

Blake is talking about connecting with your deepest yearnings, getting clear on what those are, and setting an intention that they will come. At the heart of his process of creating intentions is taking time each day to be "quiet"—akin to prioritizing empty time on a daily basis. Operating with that clarity of intention earned this very masculine guy $100 million when he exited his company! The qualities and strengths of the feminine—in both women and men—are *powerful*.

GETTING GOOD AT EMPTY TIME

As we've been exploring, empty time means making space in your life to feel the beating of your own heart—carving out concentrated time for the sole purpose of well-being, positivity, relaxation, peace, and connection to something greater than ourselves. What could be better? Let's also explore what empty time doesn't mean. It doesn't mean procrastinating, avoiding, or being lazy. It doesn't mean watching your favorite show with a bag of potato chips, or emptying out the dishwater. It doesn't even mean going on a vacation, like a safari in Africa—although that has other benefits, and personally I am looking forward to a safari one day. Empty time takes conscious awareness, inviting you to focus and direct your thoughts and attention *inside of yourself.* You actually don't need to travel anywhere to get there.

Perhaps you already take time in your life for emptiness. If you do, I'm sure this chapter just confirmed what you already know. Great job. I bet you are a positive example to other women in your life of the importance of taking time out. But if this is new to you or if you need a bit more help in this area, let me share with you some ideas on how to make empty time some of your favorite time.

YOUR EMPTY TIME FIELD GUIDE

Three Doorways for Entry:

Meditation
Nature
Retreat Time

Meditation

First, let's take some pressure off if the word "meditation" elicits any stress, like fearing that it's too hard or too boring. I've been a meditator for over thirty years, and my experience still varies. There are times when I feel total bliss and forget I am even there, and there are times that my mind doesn't stop racing. But even when my mind isn't stopping, there is still a feeling of peace. Even thoughts can't keep me from it. Please know that no matter where you fall on the spectrum of mind activity, you are doing something good for yourself.

I find that the best time to meditate is first thing in the morning. To make it easy for myself, I just sit up in bed right after waking up and meditate right there and then. Regarding how long to meditate, I suggest between ten to thirty minutes. It's up to you. The purpose is to connect, and the length is not important.

I like to think of meditation as simply taking a vacation from the mind (and sometimes *with* the mind), and here are four ways to vacation.

1. **Meditation on the heart.** Think of something you love. It can be a pet, a person, a flower, the Divine, or something else that matters to you with your whole heart. Put your attention on your heart and let the feeling of love wash over you. Enjoy the feeling, however it moves within you—accompanied by sweetness, tenderness, intensity, or joy. Imagine the love growing and filling your entire being.

2. **Meditation on the breath.** Inhale slowly and exhale slowly. Make your exhale longer than your inhale. Breathe in for three seconds, exhale for four, and repeat. Keep your concentration on your breathing. Feel your breath moving through your nose. Is it warm, cool, or tingly? Notice how it fills your body. Give your breath your gratitude for the life it helps you to live.

3. **Meditation with a chant or mantra.** Words are powerful. Repeat a mantra or chant over and over. Keep your attention on the words you are repeating. You can say the words out loud or silently inside of yourself. Here are just a few examples:

Om
I am peace
I am love
Thank you

4. **Visualization.** Imagine a beautiful, safe, and secret place just for you. Visualize a place that's either indoors or outdoors, and imagine what the doorway to this special place looks like. Open the door and be greeted by your wise self. Take her by the hand and find somewhere to sit together where you can ask her for help and guidance. While in your safe place, think about what it is that you really want and long for—imagining you already have it. What does it feel like to have what you've wanted? Enjoy this feeling and enjoy being in your safe place. Thank your wise self for her support and love.

Be Alone in Nature

The power of nature is profound. Its beauty is beyond the words we have to describe it. The colors and textures, the movement of the trees, the designs of the clouds, and the sweetness and fullness of fresh air—putting ourselves in the midst of this can ease and even absorb our worries, fears, and other negative thoughts, lifting them off us the way a bee takes the pollen from a flower and brings it to the hive to make honey.

Spend time in nature. Silence your phone, and don't listen to music. Just be in nature. Walk with awareness of the sounds, colors, fragrances, and the quality of the air. Allow nature to absorb anything—a thought or feeling—that isn't serving you. Notice how it calms you and gives you peace. Concentrate on feeling the earth under you. Find a quiet place to sit and inhale the colors through your eyes. As you rest for a little while in the arms of nature, become aware of the open place of receptivity within you.

Go on Retreats

The more time we give to emptiness, the more it rewards us. It is a powerful experience to step away from our usual surroundings and spend time in a retreat environment that fully supports non-doing and emptiness. When my husband and I go to our New Mexico retreat each summer, usually for a minimum of five weeks, it feels like a summer camp for grown-ups. We eat simply, sleep in a tent in the woods, meditate, dance, breathe, read, and sleep. Since I'm an online entrepreneur, I take my business with me, and by devoting approximately five hours per week to it, I'm able to manage it while on the retreat. This yearly tradition is one of the best things I "do" (or don't do, as it were) for the enhancement and enrichment of my whole life.

There are many retreats offered around the world that last a shorter time, such as a week or even a weekend. No matter how short or long, I know you will find the results *very* powerful. Within the emptiness, we find everything that really matters to us in body, mind, and spirit.

QUICK REVIEW

Let's recap where we are.

- Key #1 is all about really wanting what you want and getting clear on your burning desires and yearnings.
- Key #2 is where you get super focused and understand that multitasking will not bring you the success you want.
- Key #3 is about igniting your passion for growth and transformation and becoming the ferocious learner who does not hesitate to hire coaches, take courses, join a mastermind group, attend online or in-person conferences, listen to podcasts, and read powerful books.
- Key #4 is about mastering your thoughts because it is your thinking that will determine the success of your business.

- Key #5 is taking inner and outer action steps in your business.
- Key #6 is understanding and accepting that setbacks and failures are part of how successful businesses are built.
- And last, Key #7 is the surprising secret that taking empty time—non-doing time—will grow or improve your business in miraculous ways.

WHERE WE'RE GOING NEXT

Turn the page to find out why this is *your* time.

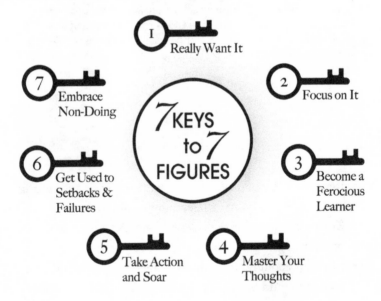

ℰ Chapter 11 ℐ

WOMEN, IT'S TIME TO RISE

"It is never too late to be what you might have been."
—GEORGE ELIOT

Now that we've reached the final chapter, I'd like to tell you the deeper reason I have written this book. After reaching seven figures in my business, buying a gorgeous apartment with Heinz, and giving myself a take-home salary of $20,000 a month *after* taxes (yes, this is all possible for you too!), I started to notice a gnawing feeling growing inside of me. Something wanted my attention, but what was it?

I took some time for inner reflection and that "something" became clear. I had spent several years building Back from Bali, and I was feeling *invisible.* Most of my time was spent behind my computer screen, working on my business. For the most part, this had suited me just fine for a long while. Even though I might not appear this way to the outside world, I am an introvert. I need a lot of alone time and being with people makes me feel more tired than energized. (Sorry, people, nothing personal.) My happy place is being with Heinz or one other friend, or taking a walk by myself in nature. (I know you other introverts can relate.)

However, there was a growing desire within me that was bigger than introversion or extroversion. I knew I had more to offer the world than bathing suit cover-ups (a popular Back from Bali product). I was feeling the rumble of *that*. I was yearning to share the knowledge I had gathered and the gift I'd been given. I was starting to feel an ache inside to share the lessons I've learned as an entrepreneur, as a woman in business, and from the many losses, challenges, and joys I've experienced in my personal life. Yet, I wasn't doing any of that.

I felt like I was hidden and muted, and it created feelings of envy and even jealousy inside of me, I am embarrassed to say. When I saw other women speaking on stages and being invited to be part of online summits on the topic of how to be successful as a women entrepreneur, I felt angry. Some of my thoughts reflected this frustration and anger clearly:

Why aren't they asking me?

She didn't even do as well as I did!

I've been doing this so much longer!

Why am I being passed over?

Why am I so invisible?

Maybe no one likes me.

Maybe I don't have anything to offer.

As I'm writing this, I need to catch my breath. And if this subject strikes a chord with you, you may need to take a deep breath too. I'm not thrilled right now about being this transparent and feeling so exposed, but I'm doing it anyway. I want to be honest with you because I know I'm not the only woman who has felt angry and frustrated about feeling invisible and passed over. If you related to this, let's get it out, shall we? Because I do get you. I know how painful it feels to have something inside of you that is yearning to be shared and yet it isn't being shared. It stirs up all of our negative thoughts and lack of confidence, and it throws us into a repetitive cycle of feeling invisible. We feel ashamed of the "ugly" feelings, and some part of us wants to remain invisible until we get ourselves sorted out.

The clincher for me came when I was having hot chocolate with my friend Ellen in one of Zurich's wonderful cafés. As I was putting the whipped cream into the thick hot chocolate, Ellen said, "Oh, I got a call from the American Women's Club, and they asked me to teach a writing workshop for their annual workshop week." At that moment, I was not sure where the steam was coming from—my hot chocolate or the top of my head.

Again? I thought. *No one ever asks ME to give a workshop.*

I went home after not enjoying that luscious hot chocolate, feeling bad for myself and armed with further proof that no one sees me, no one realizes my gifts, no one thinks I have anything to offer. A short time later, and mercifully, an unexpected and interesting thought came into my head.

Why don't YOU offer to give a workshop?

It was another turning-point moment for me.

I was suddenly ablaze with ideas and energy. In a matter of one hour, I created an outline for the workshop I mentioned earlier titled How to Start an Amazon Business and Make Money Anywhere. After writing it up, I emailed it to the organizer of the American Women's Club workshop week and immediately received a response that they *loved* the topic and thanked me for offering it. And do you know what? The workshop I gave ended up being the most popular and well-attended workshop they had ever offered.

This book that you are reading, or listening to, is one of the results of that one action I took. When I stopped waiting to be found and discovered and took action to design and offer that workshop, it kicked off a domino effect. It began a series of activities and other actions that led me to manifest my yearning to be visible and share what I know. And now, here you are!

YOUR UNSUNG SONG

Dr. Claire Zammit has a fabulous name for the affliction I just described. She calls this the Unsung Song Syndrome. For each of us, our unsung song is the feeling inside when our gifts and talents are being largely hidden rather than being expressed. The accompanying feelings of disappointment, frustration, jealousy, or sadness stem from knowing we have so much to give but are allowing fear to run the show instead.

The unsung song malaise comes from knowing we're not giving all we're capable of, and we're not realizing our highest potential. We're settling for feeling bad, self-pity, and false safety instead of possibility and faith in the power that has manifested all of the wonderment of life.

Can you relate? Is there music within you that remains unsung at this moment in your life?

Most of the women I know feel a yearning to bring forth all that is inside of them—to express their gifts and to contribute in some authentic and meaningful way to the lives of others. That's why we like to talk to each other so much. It's in talking that we help ignite and stoke the inner flame of our purpose for each other. In a million different ways, we ask each other, *What do you yearn for with your entire being?*

But so many of us work in ways that do not support bringing out our gifts—singing our song. This is at the heart of why there are so many women now looking toward entrepreneurship as a way to express their yearnings and burning desires. Women want to build and run businesses that will give them money and freedom *and* opportunities to give their gifts and offer value. We are artists, organizational consultants, therapists, bodyworkers, vegan chefs, financial advisors, inventors, designers of a million different things, and teachers of countless forms of expertise.

As Dr. Zammit says, "Women don't just want more stuff or status. We want to become all that we can be. We don't want to just succeed where men have succeeded—the traditional way that success has been defined in our world. We are yearning for the higher possibility of who we are." I know for me, that "yearning for the higher possibility" *was* that gnawing feeling that demanded my attention and moved me into action in new ways.

LET DESPERATION TURN INTO INSPIRATION

It's time, beautiful woman. It's time for you to take the actions in your life that will enable you to bring forth what you yearn for. It's time for you to rise above the limitations of the past and rise to meet your unbound self. But your rising will only come when you take action toward what you want. No one is going to do this for you. Sadly, there is no email right now in your inbox announcing that you have finally been given all you desire. Believe me, I was looking for that email for years. No matter how brilliant you are, no matter if you have figured out the mysteries of the universe, it will all remain your big secret if you don't take the risk to share it. Since you're reading this book, I'm going to assume you're not going to be satisfied by living with the secret of *you* unshared—with your song unsung. The world is full of people with great ideas who never act on them and great wisdom they share with only a few select people. But that doesn't have to be you. Make a commitment right now that you will act on your knowing and your yearnings!

We hear the words "manifestation" and "manifesting" a lot in the transformational field. Manifesting essentially means bringing something tangible into your life through belief. After much experimentation and exploration, I finally understand the essential elements to manifesting. All the vision boarding, brainstorming, list-making, meditating, and concentrating on what you want are only parts of the puzzle. There are two more pieces that are outrageously powerful for manifesting something you want: (1) do physical actions in the world, and (2) feel and act *as if it has already happened.*

In my case, way back when I didn't want to work for someone else, I jumped on a plane and created and manifested my own job by selling clothing at a street fair. When I was feeling invisible, I created and manifested the Amazon workshop so I could teach and inspire. Was I ready to do any of this? Did I know back then how to import clothing? No. Did I know how to teach a workshop or if anyone would attend? No again. The secret was and is in taking action anyway.

As I'm sure you've experienced, most of us go through periods when there's a fine line between desperation and inspiration when it comes to the feelings that are dominating our thoughts and choices. There is nothing wrong if you're currently at a place where that line is even a little blurry. For now, you can let either or both of those energies catapult you into action. In time, desperation will be wholly transformed into inspiration. As we explored in Chapter 8, your actions will simply give expression to the person you want to be and choose to be.

YOUR INNER GLASS CEILING

Okay, you say, *I'm ready! I'm ready to rise. Ready to make the money I always wanted. Ready to offer the world something valuable.* Fantastic! Now, because you've arrived at this life-changing threshold, I do have a word of warning. During this time of rising, it is quite possible you might bump up against something that derails you. It's called your inner glass ceiling. This is the invisible barrier made up of limiting thoughts and beliefs that can sabotage you from rising higher. Each of us will, at some point or another (or many times over), hit our own inner glass ceiling. Let's talk about what the ceiling may be comprised of so you'll be well prepared. Although there are many factors that can play a part, let's discuss two of the most common:

- The impostor syndrome
- Your shifting identity

The impostor syndrome is an internal belief that you are not as competent as others perceive you to be coupled with the gnawing fear that you will one day be found out. You will be unmasked, humiliated, and rejected, or so the voice of fear insists.

Remember the meditation camp I had mentioned, where I met Heinz? After attending a few summer camps, the teacher suggested to me that when I go back to New York, I should start teaching the meditation technique I had learned. *What? I thought. Me??? I'm not a spiritual teacher. I'm flawed. And I'm still very attached to potato chips!* Then the teacher said something that quickly shifted me out of my ego. He said, "Someone who knows *five* things can teach someone who knows *four*."

I can't tell you how much that statement has helped me in my life since then, and I'm hoping it is going to help you too. It showed me I don't need to be an infallible expert or the greatest spiritual teacher in the world (or some other version of the ego's idea of perfection); I just need to teach someone one more thing than they already know. It took so much pressure off me.

Denise Duffield-Thomas, in her book *Chillpreneur: The New Rules for Creating Success, Freedom and Abundance on Your Terms*, said the most popular blog post she had written at that time was titled, "Be a Contributor, Not a Guru." The focus was on giving yourself permission to contribute to the conversations you're passionate about—which may very well have to do with the work you do—and in that way, be collaborating and cocreating rather than competing and trying to hold on to a position.

"Who cares," Denise says, "if you don't know everything? Your experiences are valuable, your opinions are useful, and someone out there needs what you have. Remember you are an expert to someone." How cool is that? Don't your shoulders feel a bit lighter and relaxed now? You don't have to be the best; you just have to go and do it.

ALWAYS REMEMBER...

"There are people less qualified than you, doing the things you want to do simply because they decided to believe in themselves. Period."

(No one knows who originally said this, but it is found all over the internet because it's a potent antidote for the impostor syndrome.)

YOUR CHANGING IDENTITY

Guess what? When you become successful, whatever that means to you—you hit six, seven, or eight figures in annual revenue, you become a public speaker even though you're introverted, you move somewhere remote and start a permaculture farm, or all of the above—you may appear to be a different person to everyone who has known you. Some might be surprised and some will be delighted, but all of them will notice—and a few will be uncomfortable with the change or flat out won't like it. They'll want the old you back.

The variety of reactions can run the gamut of feelings and opinions.

When my dad listened to a podcast I was interviewed on, he said to me, "Was that my daughter?" He was both proud and amazed, as my identity as the sweet daughter had taken on greater complexity.

When my company was featured in a magazine, a friend of mine said, "I'm shocked you've done this well. I had no idea." Why be so shocked?

Sara, the founder of a public speaking training company, posted a video launching her new project, and an old friend from her past commented negatively. Why? Probably because the friend did not like or recognize this new, more visible Sara. "I will *not* dim my light!!!" Sara had told me after sharing the post. Good on you, Sara!

As your identity is changing—expanding, growing, becoming more unlimited—it can be scary and uncomfortable. We women want to belong. Belonging to something means we are not just liked, but we are safe too. Belonging is crucial to our sense of security, and study after study has proven that having close relationships is a criterion for happiness. When our identity changes, others might not see us as belonging anymore to *their* group, or *their* idea of what family members are, or *their* kind of friends. Spouses may even question if this is how *their* wife should be acting.

Let me ask you this: if you have a wildly successful business, will it conflict with your identity as a mother or as a wife or with your idea of what a woman should be? What were you taught about motherhood and being a working mother? What will your friends think of you if you get rich—like really, really rich? What will your family members think or do? I know these questions can be uncomfortable to contemplate, but it's important to acknowledge that your most important relationships may be impacted by your success.

It's not only other people's perceptions that can derail you from rising. More than any other person in the world, the way *you* think about your changing identity can also derail you if you don't look within as you grow.

I ask you now to bring honesty, curiosity, heart, and awareness to asking yourself questions like the following:

Who are you when you're not...

- Dependent
- Financially strapped
- Uncertain
- Weak
- A little girl

But instead...

- Independent
- Financially secure
- Empowered
- Strong

- An adult woman

Even the most capable and effective women feel uncertain and small at times. And women who are financially struggling and reliant on another to make ends meet certainly may be firmly seated in their adult selves. This isn't a matter of being fixed in one place or another. But asking probing questions of yourself can help you shine a light on tendencies and on ways of being that have become comfort zones that prevent you from rising. So let's really go for it, shall we?

Who are you when you are no longer hiding?

Who are you when you no longer *need* to be married or in partnership solely for financial reasons?

Your own shining awareness of *yourself*—of who you have been and who you're becoming—will allow you to beautifully dismantle your inner glass ceiling instead of allowing it to come crashing down. Therefore, I invite you to investigate from the highest place within you—and not as a way to critique yourself but as a way to generously clear the way for your ever-evolving success and happiness.

LEAP INTO THE POSSIBILITIES

I know it can feel frustrating to be told that we, as enterprising women, have never had more opportunities than we have now while we still feel like we haven't quite joined the ranks. We might feel like some possibilities still remain largely out of reach. If you are still struggling to reach the success you want, give yourself a break. In many ways, this is new territory. It's still astounding to consider that before 1974, women in the United States were not allowed to get their own credit card without their husband's permission, and unmarried women were outright refused. We can't even imagine this today, but many of us reading this book were alive when this was happening. It was not that long ago. But the truth is, we *do* have more possibilities and options, and the statistics confirm it:

- Women own 12.3 million businesses in the United States.
- Women-owned businesses in the United States generate $1.8 trillion a year (source: Women's Business Enterprise National Council).
- Forty percent of businesses in the United States are women-owned (source: Women's Business Enterprise National Council).
- In 2020, women started 1,821 new businesses *per day*. Of that number, 64 percent were owned by women of color.
- Over the last five years, the number of women-owned businesses increased 21 percent, while all businesses increased only 9 percent.
- Entrepreneurs applied for federal tax ID numbers to register 4.54 million new businesses from January through October 2021, up 56 percent from the same period of 2019 according to Census Bureau data (source: *The Wall Street Journal* in an article titled "Workers Quit Jobs in Droves to Become Their Own Bosses," https://www.wsj.com/articles/workers-quit-jobs-in-droves-to-become-their-own-bosses-11638199199).
- Sixty percent of people who start small businesses (women and men) are between forty and sixty years old, and the average age of a small business owner is 50.3 (source: Guidant Financial). Once again, that it is never too late.

It's true, our powers are rising. More and more women are stepping into entrepreneurship in order to take control over their lives, make money, take care of their families, contribute their skills and talents in ways that feel valuable to them, and live the lives they want.

YOU CAN RISE ABOVE THE NUMBER ONE REASON FOR BUSINESS CLOSURES

As you know, having a business does not necessarily mean keeping a business. Lack of profitability, not access to capital, according to the Global Entrepreneurship Monitor, is the number one reason cited by both men and women for closing the doors on their businesses. This is why women need the business skills that help them not only make money but keep money—and ultimately, invest money.

In short, always remember, you are in the money business. And when you temporarily forget, reread Chapter 3.

WHAT KIND OF LIFE DO YOU WANT?

If you know deep inside that you can be doing better than you are doing now—if you know you want to earn more money, have more freedom, step into your greatest self, share your gifts, serve in the form of offering great products or fabulous programs to help others—then it's time to say yes to yourself. Remember, as we explored in Chapter 4, one of the softest, easiest, and yet most powerful ways you can do this begins with these two words: "I wonder." Wonder out loud in the bathroom mirror. Wonder while you're driving your car. Wonder in your journal. Wonder while you're taking a morning walk. Wonder in conversation with a deeply trusted soul sister.

I wonder what would happen if I quit my job?

I wonder what would happen if I started a business?

I wonder what would happen if I changed my product line?

I wonder what would happen if I created a digital course?

I wonder how I could impact my industry if I wrote a book? Or how many lives I could positively influence?

I wonder how my life would change if I did the things I've been thinking and dreaming about?

I wonder what exciting opportunities await me that I've never even considered?

I wonder how having an abundance of money, freedom, and success will feel?

I wonder _____ *?*

You deserve to find out what's on the other side of your wonderings. You deserve success. You deserve to feel good about yourself. You deserve to enjoy being your fully empowered self. And you deserve to step into the greatest possibility of who you are.

With your very first breath, you were given the sweetest gift, and that gift is your yearning to express who you are and to share your gifts. The world wants your gifts; the world wants your success. It may not consciously know that it wants what you have, but when it receives it, there will be a collective "thank you"—thank you for not holding back.

"When a great ship is in harbor and moored, it is safe, there can be no doubt. But…that is not what great ships are built for," says author Clarissa Pinkola Estés. You, magnificent woman, are the great ship. You are bound for extraordinary adventures—in the world and along the waterways of your own heart.

So what kind of life *do* you want to have? Ultimately, that is the question you need to ask yourself. I personally believe we have a responsibility to ourselves, to those around us, to our souls, and to the universe itself to bring forth our gifts. To do so is how we put our love in action. It's how we love life.

Ultimately, stepping into our rising is a decision based on self-value and self-love. When we don't stand up for what we know we can do, we are undervaluing ourselves, which means we're not loving ourselves. "There is nothing enlightened about shrinking so that other people won't feel insecure around you. We are all meant to shine, as children do," says Marianne Williamson.

When you are lying on your deathbed, how will you feel about your choices? I know this is an uncomfortable question to think about, but as I've shared with you, death has been a close friend in my life and I know the reality of it, as many of you do too. Every moment matters, and every moment is a new beginning. Why not start now?

You know as do I that it's all about the journey, not the destination. The journey toward success can bring you ongoing opportunities to learn, grow, share what you've learned, and have a grand time expressing yourself while contributing to others. This is the power of being an entrepreneur. There is no one great end result. The "result" is ongoing—*it's who you are becoming while you are on this journey*. It's who you are always and forever becoming because there is no end. There is only rising.

And remember, it's time. It's our time as women living in a world of unprecedented need and possibility. And it is your time. Right. Now.

Let us see you rise.

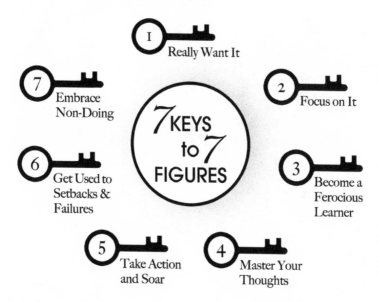

ACKNOWLEDGMENTS

As the great Sufi poet Rumi said, "The divine enters through our wounds." If there is one thing I know for sure, it is that the difficulties in our life bring the greatest transformation and opportunity for healing and growth. With that in mind, I thank and acknowledge the challenges and losses I have experienced, as I would not be who I am without them.

Nor would I be who I am without the people in my life whose shoulders I stand on, those who have supported me through the good and challenging times, and who have given me the most precious gift of all—love.

To my amazing, colorful, inspiring, fun, and dynamic family for giving me unconditional love and extraordinary support throughout my life. I was raised to honor family, and to me, family is truly everything. My beloved dad, Norman, passed, but he would have been incredibly proud of this book. He was a seeker, a ferocious learner, an entrepreneur, generous to everyone, and he showered me with love. My mom, Carol, who is also an entrepreneur, is a great inspiration to me every day.

She is a singer, author, and a woman of enormous courage and independence. Thank you, Mom, for always being there for me. And then there are my brothers, Eric and Roger, whom I love so much it almost hurts. Eric, what a creative, dynamic spirit you are, and Roger, with your soft heart and inner wisdom. I'm so lucky to have you as my brothers. You guys mean more to me than you know. To my aunts, cousins, and cousins-related-to-my-cousins; to my nieces, nephews, my sisters-in-law and all their children—I love you all so very much.

To Kristine Carlson, without her, this book would not be in your hands. I was introduced to Kristine shortly after my dad passed in 2019. It was a poignant and sad time for me, and her Book Doulas' Incubator program came at the right time. I always knew I would write a book, and over the last few years I had been ablaze with a burning desire to share what I've learned as an entrepreneur. Kristine's program seemed destined. I had good intentions when I began the course, but because of needing to travel to Bali for my business, I just couldn't take part in the program. Despite my good intentions and my desire to write a book, it got dropped by the wayside. But that all changed in April 2020. During COVID-19 lockdown, Kris reached out to me to let me know that another incubator was about to start, and she generously offered me to retake the course. And so began my second chance. I am forever grateful to Kris, who possesses a rare depth of experience in the transformational author field. Thank you for being a champion and passionate supporter of me and my work.

To the extraordinary Debra Evans, my editor (and the other half of Book Doulas), whose abilities to marry writing skill with intuition are genius. There are truly no words to thank Debra for the dedication and commitment she gave me, week after week and month after month, during our many Zoom calls. Not only did we dive into the depths of the book, but we also dived deep into mutually appreciating each other. Her passionate and unwavering belief in the ideas in this book, and in me, was a gift that kept me going and gave me the confidence to be as vulnerable with you as I have been in my writing. Our greatest desire as humans is to feel seen as someone of value. Debra did that for me, and I'm eternally grateful. Deb, you made writing this book one of the happiest times of my life.

To my teachers, mentors, consultants, authors, and spiritual teachers who have guided me and have had a profound influence on my life. In particular, to Lisa Suttora, my business consultant who saw my potential way before I ever did and who has assisted me on this journey to become a multimillion-dollar business owner. To Ali Brown, who taught me to think outside of the box and through her workshops, introduced me to many inspiring and powerful women entrepreneurs. To Dr. Claire Zammit, who changed my life with her renowned Feminine Power course. To Ryan Daniel Moran, whose authenticity and vulnerability, especially pertaining to having an 8-Figure Exit, inspires me greatly. Thank you for teaching me the secret to wealth, which is to build a business and invest the profits. To Ingrid Vanderveldt, who lit a fire inside of me when I first heard her speak, who called me to *rise*. And to Adnan Sarhan, my spiritual teacher, who gave me the gift of the inner life.

To my dear friends—old friends, new friends, Sufi friends, friends who are more like family, and friends who have passed. You know who you are and how much each of you mean to me. Thank you for always being there for me. I love each of you.

To the many women entrepreneurs I interviewed for this book, thank you for generously giving me your time and your insights. You will find your wisdom throughout this book.

To the Pandemic Book Club Ladies (yep, that is what we call ourselves) who were part of my Book Doulas writing group and who gave me sisterhood and so much support.

To the people of Bali, Indonesia, who welcomed me into their land and hearts and who have been my partners for over thirty years. Sharing your beautiful handicrafts and art has been the foundation of my business.

To the animals in my life—Gaylord, Icarus, Cleopatra, and Bearli, all who have passed. Thank you for sitting next to me through all the ups and downs of life and loving me, and blasting my heart open repeatedly. Thinking of you reminds me that I can't wait to meet my next furry friend.

And last, to the greatest gift of all, my very best friend, my beloved husband, Heinz—the man with the biggest heart in all the world. You truly are my rock. No one knows me more deeply. You make me feel loved and seen every single day. Thank you.

MILLION DOLLAR MINDSET RESOURCES

Dear Beautiful Woman Entrepreneur,

My support for you doesn't end with this book. There are simple ways to continue to work with me, and below, you'll find my offerings, along with the specific links to my websites and social media streams.

One of my greatest joys is to be in conversation with women entrepreneurs, and I wholeheartedly invite you to utilize all of my free content—listen to my podcast, read my blog, download my free e-book, subscribe to my YouTube channels, and follow me on social media. If you feel the call, please join me for one of my online courses or schedule a consulting session.

Most of all, I would love to hear from you personally. You can reach me at Leslie@lesliekuster.com.

Wishing you the greatest success and the freedom to fly high,
Leslie

LESLIE KUSTER ONLINE

Leslie's main website

www.lesliekuster.com

FREE E-BOOK

Leslie's free eBook: *7 Mistakes Most Women Entrepreneurs Make and What to Do Instead!*

www.lesliekuster.com/7mistakes

ONLINE COURSES

Leslie's online courses

https://www.lesliekuster.com/courses/

PODCAST

Leslie's Podcasts

https://www.lesliekuster.com/podcast/

BLOG

Leslie's Money and Freedom Blog

https://www.lesliekuster.com/blog/

PRIVATE COACHING AND CONSULTING

Million Dollar Mindset mentor and consulting with Leslie

https://www.lesliekuster.com/consulting/

SOCIAL MEDIA

Leslie on Instagram

www.instagram.com/lesliekusterofficial

Leslie on Facebook

https://www.facebook.com/LeslieKusterOfficial/

Leslie on LinkedIn

www.linkedin.com/in/lesliekuster

YOUTUBE CHANNELS

Leslie on YouTube

https://www.youtube.com/channel/
UCBtp1gkqsNilja1ehn4NHHw

Back from Bali on YouTube

https://www.youtube.com/channel/
UCklUu4_hEVZR3HGuwTpcalg

BACK FROM BALI ONLINE
Back from Bali on Amazon

https://www.amazon.com/backfrombali

Back from Bali website

https://www.backfrombali.com/

ADDITIONAL RESOURCES
In addition to Leslie Kuster's resources, this section contains a rich collection of other people and tools you will find useful along your entrepreneurial journey.

WOMEN'S ENTREPRENEURSHIP AND LEADERSHIP
Ali Brown, Founder of The Trust, a private network for $1 million-plus women entrepreneurs, coach and mentor, host of top podcast *Glambition Radio*

https://alibrown.com/

Claire Zammit, PhD, Founder of Feminine Power and The Institute for Woman-Centered Coaching, Training & Leadership

https://femininepower.com/

https://evolvingwisdom.com

Ingrid Vanderveldt, Chairman and CEO of Empowering a Billion Women (EBW) and Vanderveldt Global Investments

https://ingridvanderveldt.com/

Holly Dowling, Global Keynote Speaker and Inspirational Thought Leader

https://www.hollydowling.com/

E-COMMERCE TRAINING

Lisa Suttora

https://lisasuttora.com/

Ryan Daniel Moran, Capitalism.com

https://www.capitalism.com/

Scott Voelker, Brand Creators

https://brandcreators.com/

Steve Chou, My Wife Quit Her Job

https://mywifequitherjob.com/

REAL ESTATE, FINANCE, INVESTING
Michelle Bosch, Real Estate Investing

https://www.michellebosch.com/

The Bottom Line Bookkeeping

https://www.thebottomlinecpa.com/contact/

Bookkeeping software—Xero

https://www.xero.com/us/

Ryan Daniel Moran, Capitalism.com

https://www.capitalism.com/podcasts/capitalism-com/

The Real Estate Guys Radio

https://realestateguysradio.com/

Bigger Pockets

https://www.biggerpockets.com/

MARKETING

Interview Connections, podcast booking

https://interviewconnections.com/

Amy Porterfield

https://www.amyporterfield.com/

Sigrun

https://www.sigrun.com/

Paula Rizzo, media training

https://paularizzo.com/

PERSONAL DEVELOPMENT

Don't Sweat the Small Stuff, the book series and brand, Kristine Carlson

https://dontsweat.com/

https://kristinecarlson.com/

Feminine Power, Claire Zammit, PhD

https://femininepower.com/

The Life Coaching School, Brooke Castillo

https://thelifecoachschool.com/

HIRING HELP
Upwork

https://www.upwork.com

Fiverr

https://www.fiverr.com/

Freelancer

https://www.freelancer.com/

Indeed

https://www.indeed.com/

GRAPHICS
Canva

https://www.canva.com/

Pic Monkey

https://www.picmonkey.com/

99 Designs

https://99designs.com/

RECOMMENDED BOOKS
MINDSET AND PERSONAL GROWTH:
Think and Grow Rich, Napoleon Hill

See You at the Top, Zig Ziglar

The Power of Now, Eckhart Tolle

The Five Secrets You Must Discover before You Die, John Izzo

Playing Big, Tara Mohr

The Big Leap, Gay Hendricks

The Confidence Gap, Russ Harris

FINANCE AND BUSINESS:
$100M Offers: How to Make Offers So Good People Feel Stupid Saying No, Alex Hormozi

Rich Dad Poor Dad, Robert Kiyosaki

Sacred Success, a Course in Financial Miracles, Barbara Stanny

12 Months to $1 Million, Ryan Daniel Moran

Blue Ocean Strategy, W. Chan Kim

The Take Action Approach, Scott Voelker

Profit First, Mike Michalowicz (and all of Mike's books)

Money, a Love Story, Kate Northrup

Entrepreneurial You, Dorie Clark

WOMEN AND FEMININE EMPOWERMENT:
Rise Sister Rise, Rebecca Campbell

The Moment of Lift, Melinda Gates

Playing Big, Tara Mohr

ABOUT THE AUTHOR

LESLIE KUSTER is the Million Dollar Mindset mentor and consultant for women over forty-five who want to become wildly successful entrepreneurs and fall in love with life again.

Her core message: *"It's never too late to create success, financial wealth, and a life of freedom. You're just getting started—if you choose it and want it."*

Leslie Kuster is a multiple seven-figure e-commerce brand owner, business mentor, speaker, and writer. In her mid-fifties, at an age when many women consider slowing down, she made a life-changing decision to commit to making money and building her business, taking her clothing brand, Back from Bali, from $50,000 a year in annual revenue to multiple seven figures in annual revenue. The success of Back from Bali—which offers women's bohemian-chic clothing ethically made in Bali, Indonesia—affords Leslie the life of her dreams.

Through her writing, teaching, and speaking, Leslie empowers and guides women to create businesses that align with their deepest core values, enabling them to work in ways that bring greater ease, flow, and fulfillment into their daily lives. She ignites the passion in the women she reaches through her 1:1 mentoring and coaching, podcast guesting, blog, online courses, and social platforms, showing women *how* to choose a new and extraordinary path.

With over thirty years of experience as an entrepreneur, Leslie's passion inspires women to pursue entrepreneurship as a direct path to independence and wealth. Empowering women has been a lifelong passion for Leslie. With an MSW and LCSW in clinical social work, before launching Back from Bali, Leslie was the founder and creator of Girl Power, a mind-body-spirit program for young girls, seven to thirteen years old, offering self-empowerment workshops and programs.

Trained by acclaimed transformational speaker Lisa Nichols, Leslie herself is a powerful speaker who is sought after by event organizations and podcast shows internationally. She inspires her audiences with her combination of authenticity, practical wisdom, and a sincere enthusiasm for business and life that have resulted in several awards from Toast Masters International.

Leslie lives in the United States with her Swiss husband, Heinz.